Matthew and Mark

A Relational Paraphrase

Ben Campbell Johnson

WORD BOOKS
PUBLISHER
4800 WEST WACO DRIVE
WACO, TEXAS
76703

MATTHEW AND MARK

Copyright © 1978 by Ben Campbell Johnson

ISBN 0–8499–0093–X

Library of Congress Catalog Card Number: 78-59463

Printed in the United States of America

Contents

Preface

Paraphrasing Matthew and Mark was a significant spiritual experience for me. As I read their portrait of Jesus, he became more real to me as a person than ever before, and I recognized anew the relevance and power of his teachings.

In this preface, I want to share with you my view of how these New Testament Gospels were conceived in the minds of those first followers of Jesus and how we may appropriate their truth for our lives.

Jesus is timeless in both his life and teachings. However, each generation must encounter the Jesus of history and translate the meaning of that encounter into relevant, contemporary language—a translation that expresses our relation to him.

Language is a symbolic way to express that experience. For example, a person has an experience which results in certain feelings and images on the inside. Through the use of words which symbolize that experience, he or she communicates its meaning to others.

Jesus was in touch with and experienced the depth dimension of human/divine existence, and he expressed that dimension of being by his every act. He then explained this reality in his teachings. His understudies (disciples), observing his actions and listening to his words, began to glimpse the reality of God that Jesus had come to reveal. With the guidance of the Holy Spirit, they put in writing his sayings and their interpretation of his actions. So in these Gospels, we have a report of their firsthand encounter with the Christ, and with the God and Father he revealed.

As I have read their accounts, I have tried to penetrate the symbols which Jesus used by asking, "What does he mean by this?" After getting my understanding clear, I've asked how I would express that meaning in language most applicable to my life and to my understanding of God's purpose for me. The result of this endeavor is *Matthew and Mark: A Relational Paraphrase.* (A further volume containing Luke and John is planned.)

I urge you not to judge me as seeking to pervert or distort the biblical image of Jesus. Rather, I hope you will affirm my effort to hear Jesus' message in the first century and translate it meaningfully into the twentieth century.

For example, I frequently paraphrase "disciple" as "understudy." The dictionary generally defines a "disciple" as one who adheres to the doctrines of another, but to be a disciple in the Christian sense involves much more than accepting a doctrine. It involves experiencing Christ, alive in us, utilizing all the dimensions of our person to communicate his love and care for others.

"Understudy," to me, is a more appropriate word to describe the nature of Jesus' followers. Understudy is a word I've borrowed from the theater; it refers broadly to one who is able to take on the role if the lead actor is not physically present. The understudy doesn't simply mimic or imitate; he fulfills the role—and, in a sense, that is what a disciple does. Disciples are understudies who observe the style and the words of the Leading Part in the Gospels so that they can take his part when he is not physically present. Jesus manifests himself through these understudies who take his part on earth today. He is incarnate in his followers.

Another word of explanation is in order about my frequent paraphrase of "kingdom of God" (or "kingdom of heaven") to mean "Spirit dimension." We usually think of the kingdom of God as a utopian dream that will only become reality some time in the distant future. We think of heaven as being "up there" or at least somewhere far away. "Spirit dimension," on the other hand, places an emphasis on the here and now presence of God's kingdom and activities as a reality in every experience of life.

The paraphrase of scripture is the task of each of us. In fact, every Christian paraphrases, whether consciously or unconsciously, because every time you read a verse of scripture and ask what it means, you are in that moment mentally paraphrasing.

So, I offer to you my paraphrase of the Jesus stories and teachings with the sincere hope that it will assist you in your journey of faith and in your hearing his Word to you.

Finally, I want to express my appreciation to Dr. Arthur Wainwright, Professor of New Testament at Candler School of Theology, Emory University, for his many helpful suggestions; to my able associate and editor, Harriette Griffin, for her assistance in research and editing; and to Floyd Thatcher, vice president of Word, Inc., for encouraging the continuation of this project. Lastly, my appreciation to my wife, Nan, with whom I experience Jesus in a relational way!

BEN JOHNSON

Glossary

In this book I have paraphrased certain traditional words with symbols which I hope will be meaningful in today's world. Below, I've listed some of these key terms, along with the definitive symbols which I used to paraphrase them.

angel—special messenger of God
chief priest—religious leader or official
commandments—directives
disciples—understudies
elders—rulers; decision makers for the nation
eternal life—authentic life age after age
Herodians—supporters of Herod
high priest—prominent religious official
kingdom of God (kingdom of heaven)—Spirit dimension (suggests the spiritual essence in all of life)
Pharisees—pious Rulekeepers
prophet—spokesperson for God
Sadducees—religious aristocrats (materialists and leaders of the Jewish community)
Satan—Adversary
scribes—interpreters of the rules
Son of man—Representative Man
temple—house of worship; house of God or God's house

Matthew

INTRODUCTION

First of all, although the New Testament opens with the Book of Matthew, it was not the first Gospel to be written. Mark is generally conceded to have been written first and to have served as a primary source of information for Matthew.

Second, the author of the first Gospel has generally been considered to be Matthew, the tax collector, one of Jesus' disciples, though in recent years some researchers have suggested that the author may have been a close friend or associate of his. In any case, the Book was probably written in Antioch of Syria around A.D. 80–85.

What is distinctive about the Gospel of Matthew? It has the heaviest Jewish emphasis of any Gospel, as the author stresses again and again the role of Jesus as the Messiah in fulfillment of the ancient scriptures' prophecy. In fact, the ancient scriptures are quoted more frequently in Matthew than in Mark, Luke, and John.

Matthew was also concerned with the growing Christian church and realized that Jesus' followers needed to have not only a record of his life and ministry, but also the body of his teachings from which they could draw guidelines for living. It is interesting, too, that Matthew is the only gospel writer who refers specifically to the "church" (16:18 and 18:17) or, as I have paraphrased, "a community of persons who are related to me" and "a fellowship of faith . . . the spiritual community of faith," respectively.

Note that the first refers to the universal church and the second to the local church.

The structure of Matthew follows the general outline of Jesus' life:

> chapters 1, 2—the birth of Jesus to fulfill the forecast of scripture
>
> chapters 3–20—the ministry of Jesus
>
> chapters 21–28—the last week of Jesus' life, his crucifixion, burial, and resurrection

Scattered throughout his Gospel are several concentrated areas that focus on specific subjects:

> chapters 5–9—the Sermon on the Mount
>
> chapter 10—guidelines for understudies
>
> chapter 13—stories about the Spirit dimension
>
> chapters 24, 25—the climax of history

Although Matthew's ties with Jewish history and tradition are strong and pervasive, his concluding verses plainly show that the message of the gospel is indeed for the world. The "Great Commission" (28:19, 20) is a fitting climax to a book whose roots were in prophecy, but whose aim was to go beyond those roots and present the new "community of faith" established by Jesus Christ and his followers.

THE GOSPEL OF MATTHEW

Jesus' earthly lineage

1 [1] Here is the family tree of Jesus the Christ, the son of David, the son of Abraham.

[2] Abraham fathered Isaac and Isaac fathered Jacob and Jacob fathered Judah and all his brothers. [3] Judah fathered Perez and Zerah of Tamar; and Perez fathered Hezron, and Hezron fathered Ram. [4] And Ram fathered Amminadab, and Amminadab fathered Nahshon, and Nahshon fathered Salmon. [5] And Salmon fathered Boaz through Rahab, and Boaz fathered Obed through Ruth, and Obed fathered Jesse. [6] Jesse fathered David who became our king, and then David the king fathered Solomon through the woman who had been the wife of Uriah. [7] And Solomon fathered Rehoboam, and Rehoboam fathered Abijah, and Abijah fathered Asa. [8] And Asa fathered Jehoshaphat, and Jehoshaphat fathered Joram, and Joram fathered Uzziah. [9] And Uzziah fathered Jotham, and Jotham fathered Ahaz, and Ahaz fathered Hezekiah. [10] And Hezekiah fathered Manasseh and Manasseh fathered Amos, and Amos fathered Josiah. [11] And Josiah fathered Jechoniah and his brothers about the time that our nation was taken captive into Babylon.

[12] And after our fathers were brought to Babylon, Jechoniah fathered Shealtiel, and Shealtiel fathered Zerubbabel. [13] And Zerubbabel fathered Abiud and Abiud fathered Eliakim and Eliakim fathered Azor. [14] And Azor fathered Zadok, and Zadok fathered Achim, and Achim fathered Eliud. [15] And Eliud fathered Eleazar, and Eleazar fathered Matthan, and Matthan fathered Jacob. [16] And Jacob fathered Joseph, who became the husband of Mary, who gave birth to Jesus who is called the Christ.

[17] One way to arrange the family tree of Jesus the Christ is to recognize that from Abraham to David there were fourteen generations, and from David until our nation was taken captive into Babylon there were fourteen generations, and from the time that our nation was taken into Babylon until Christ was born, there were fourteen generations.

Jesus' parents

[18] Here are the details concerning the conception of Jesus the Christ. His mother, Mary, was engaged to Joseph. Before their marriage she became pregnant through the Holy Spirit. [19] Joseph, being a compassionate person, did not wish to embarrass her publicly, so he was considering breaking their engagement quietly. [20] While he was dealing with his conflicting feelings, he had a dream which clarified his decision. In the dream a special messenger of God appeared to him and said, "Joseph, David's son, do not be anxious about your engagement to Mary. Take her for your wife because the child which she has conceived is a result of the action of the Holy Spirit. [21] She will give birth to a son whom you are to name Jesus, because he will liberate his people from all that oppresses them."

[22] These events took place in order to fulfill what one of the Lord's spokespersons had said long ago—[23] "One day, a virgin will be pregnant and will bear a son, and his name will be called 'God with us.'"

[24] When Joseph awoke, he did as the Lord's special messenger in the dream had instructed, and he married Mary. [25] But Joseph did not have intercourse with Mary until the baby was born; and as was instructed, he called his name Jesus.

Jesus' birth

2 [1] Here is the story of Jesus' birth. He was born in the town of Bethlehem in the province of Judea when Herod

was king. Herod first heard of his birth when a traveling party of astrologers from the East came to Jerusalem. ² They inquired, "Where is that person who has been born to rule the Jews? We have seen an unusual configuration of stars in the East and have come to pay our respects to him."

³ The reported birth of a ruler caused Herod to be anxious; in fact, the whole city shared his distress. ⁴ The troubled Herod gathered the religious leaders as well as the interpreters of the rules, and he inquired of them where the Christ was to be born. ⁵ Without hesitation they said, "In Bethlehem of Judea because one of our spokespersons has said, ⁶ 'And you Bethlehem, in the land of Judah, are not inferior to any of the princes of Judah because from you shall come a leader who will govern all the people of Israel.' "

⁷ After his conference with these leaders, Herod held a private conference with the astrologers and asked them at what specific time they had seen the astral configuration. ⁸ At the conclusion of their conference, Herod dispatched them to Bethlehem saying, "You go and search high and low for this child. When you have found him, bring your report back to me so that I may pay my respects to him also."

⁹ With that word from the king, the astrologers departed. To their amazement, the star which they had seen in their own country appeared again and guided them directly to the baby. ¹⁰ The reappearance of the phenomenon in the heavens overjoyed them.

¹¹ The astrologers entered the house and found the baby with Mary, his mother. They fell to their knees to worship him, opened their bags and offered their gifts: gold, incense, and spices.

¹² After seeing the baby, the astrologers had a dream in which God instructed them not to report back to Herod, but rather to return to their homes by another route.

¹³ After their departure, one of God's special messengers

[15

spoke again to Joseph in a dream, saying, "Get up and take the baby and his mother and go into Egypt. Stay there until I call you to return because Herod will endeavor to destroy the child." [14] Joseph got up during the night and departed with his family for Egypt. [15] They remained there until the death of Herod so that the ancient prediction could be fulfilled which said: "Out of Egypt I have called my son."

Herod's cruel deed

[16] After Herod had waited a number of months for the return of the astrologers, it became obvious to him that they would bring him no information concerning the birth of Jesus. Insane with anger, he sent his soldiers into Bethlehem and the surrounding countryside with instructions to kill all the male children two years old and under. His calculation concerning the child's age was based on the time that the astrologers had first visited him. [17] This act also concurs with what the ancients had predicted would happen. God's spokesman Jeremiah said, [18] "In Ramah, there was heard a loud voice of weeping and crying and deep mourning. Rachel, a mother, wept for her children and would let no one comfort her because they were all taken away."

[19] When Herod died, a special messenger of the Lord again spoke to Joseph in a dream while he was living in Egypt. [20] The messenger said, "Get up and take your son and his mother and go back into the land of Israel because the king who sought to destroy him is dead."

[21] So Joseph got up, took the boy and his mother, and came back to his native land of Israel. [22] Upon his arrival, he heard that Archelaus, Herod's son, was governing the land in the place of his father. This news frightened Joseph, and once again God spoke to him in a dream, instructing him to depart into Galilee. [23] So Joseph settled in the town of Nazareth. This decision was also predicted by one of the ancients who said, "He shall be called a Nazarene."

16]

John the Baptizer's ministry

3 ¹ A number of years later, John the Baptizer, by his own witness in the deserts of Judea, announced the beginning of Jesus' ministry. ² He said to everyone who would listen, "Change your attitudes and your actions. Prepare yourself for an invasion of the Spirit dimension which is imminent."

³ For the information of you Jews, this Baptizer was forecast by Isaiah, one of our ancient writers, when he said, "There will be the voice of a person witnessing in the desert: get ready for the coming of the one who fully embodies the Spirit dimension. Clearly mark his way."

⁴ Now this Baptizer lived an ascetic life. He wore a vest of camel's hair and a leather belt. He ate the fruit of the locust tree mixed with wild honey. ⁵ Both his witnessing and his strange manner attracted crowds from Jerusalem and the whole countryside of Judea around the river Jordan. ⁶ Many of those who listened to his testimony submitted themselves to his baptism and acknowledged the sinfulness of their attitudes and actions.

⁷ On one occasion when the Baptizer noted a number of both the pious Rulekeepers and the religious aristocrats in his audience, he addressed them directly: "You deceptive and cunning religious leaders, who has awakened you to the impending invasion of the Spirit? Who has warned you about God's coming? ⁸ If you intend to participate in the imminent spiritual invasion, demonstrate a change in your attitude and actions. ⁹ Do not offer this rationalization: 'We are the offspring of Abraham and need nothing more.' I say to you, God can make sons out of stones if he so chooses and need not depend upon the so-called descendants of Abraham. ¹⁰ I forewarn you that the woodcutter is already swinging his axe at the very root of the trees. Every tree in this forest which does not produce good fruit will be cut down and burned. ¹¹ When you give evidence of a change in attitude and behavior, I can then baptize you with water. But my baptism is but a symbol.

Yes, the one who is about to appear is superior to me, and I do not feel worthy to unlace his shoes. He has the true baptism of which mine is but a preparation. He will baptize you with the Holy Spirit, and his baptism will ignite the depths of your being. ¹² The one of whom I speak carries a separator with him, and with it he separates the wheat from the chaff. And he will gather the wheat for storage, but he will burn up the chaff with a blazing fire."

Jesus is baptized

¹³ Sometime after the Baptizer's pronouncement to the religious leaders, Jesus came from his home in Galilee to Judea to that region of the Jordan where John was baptizing. He asked John to baptize him. ¹⁴ John was appalled at Jesus' request and resisted him, saying, "I really need to have you baptize me. Why do you ask me to baptize you?" ¹⁵ Jesus responded, "Go ahead and baptize me, John, because I must fulfill God's purpose by identifying with all the people."

At this, John baptized Jesus. ¹⁶ The baptism was a peak experience for Jesus. After John had administered the baptism, Jesus came immediately out of the water and heaven was opened up to him, and the very essence of the Spirit of God came upon him like a dove flying through the sky. ¹⁷ And in the midst of this ecstasy, he heard a voice from heaven saying, "You are my much beloved son; in you I take great pride."

The Adversary tests Jesus

4 ¹ Sometime after this revelation which was given to Jesus at his baptism, the Spirit directed him into the desert to face the testings of the Adversary. ² In preparation for his testing, Jesus abstained from food and drink for forty days. After that, he was hungry. ³ Then the Adversary came to him with the first test. "If you really are the Son of God, as the voice said at your baptism, transform these stones into food."

⁴ Jesus responded, "A human being cannot exist on the

physical necessities alone, but must be sustained by spiritual resources."

⁵ The Adversary then set the stage for the second test. He took Jesus into the city of Jerusalem and placed him on the uppermost part of the Jewish house of God. ⁶ He then said to him again, "If you are the Son of God, jump from this height. Surely you can trust the ancient scriptures which say, 'God will send his special messengers to catch you lest you injure yourself.' "

⁷ Jesus answered calmly, "It is also written, 'You shall not force God to prove himself.' "

⁸ For the third test, the Adversary placed Jesus on a high mountain and pointed to all the various seats of power in the world. ⁹ And he said to Jesus, "I will give you all of these and the adulation which goes with them, if you will give your adoration to me."

¹⁰ Jesus said to him, "Get away from me, Adversary, because our ancients have written, 'You will worship the Lord God and give your complete adoration to him.' " ¹¹ With that rebuke, the Adversary departed from Jesus, and special messengers from God comforted and encouraged him.

Isaiah's prophecy fulfilled

¹² Sometime after the great temptation, Jesus learned that John the Baptizer had been apprehended and put in jail. ¹³ Upon learning this, Jesus left Nazareth and went into Galilee. He set up his headquarters in Capernaum, a seacoast town in the region of Zebulun and Naphtali. ¹⁴ This choice fulfills the prediction which was made by Isaiah: ¹⁵ "The region of Zebulun and Naphtali which is by the sea, across the Jordan, next to Galilee, where live a number of non-Jews— ¹⁶ the people who live in meaninglessness and despair have glimpsed reality and those whose lives have bordered on death have tasted real life."

¹⁷ From the time that John was in prison, Jesus began his

ministry saying to all the people, "Change your attitude and actions because an invasion of the Spirit is imminent."

Jesus calls four understudies

[18] Soon after Jesus began proclaiming the invasion of the Spirit dimension, he also began to invite certain persons to become his special understudies and to participate in his mission. Jesus began gathering these associates one day when he was walking by the Sea of Galilee and met Simon who is called Peter, and his brother, Andrew, busy about their fishing. [19] He said to them, "Join yourselves to me and be part of my mission, and you will pull people's lives out of meaninglessness and despair just as you are pulling fish from the sea." [20] Without any hesitation, they dropped what they were doing and joined him. [21] As Jesus walked on down the beach, he saw two brothers, James and John, with their father Zebedee, repairing their nets. Interrupting their labors, Jesus invited the brothers to participate with him in his ministry. [22] Without any hesitation, they, too, dropped their work, got out of the boat, said goodbye to their father, and joined Jesus.

News about Jesus spreads

[23] In the early days of his ministry, Jesus went throughout Galilee explaining his message in the meeting places of the Jews and talking about the good news of the Spirit invasion. His descriptions were accompanied by the healing of all kinds of sicknesses and diseases which the people had. [24] News of these healings spread rapidly throughout all of Syria, and persons from all quarters brought him sick people with various kinds of diseases—neurotics tormented with anxiety, those who were separated from their true selves, those who were emotionally sick, and those who were paralyzed. Jesus made all of these persons whole. [25] The crowds swelled as news of his healings attracted large groups from Galilee, from the ten cities, from Jerusalem, from Judea, and from that region across the Jordan River. The crowds gathered both to see

what he would do to the sick and to hear what he had to say about life.

Attaining fulfillment

5 ¹ On these occasions when large crowds gathered, Jesus would make his way up into a mountain and his understudies would join him. ² Here is a summary of the things which he taught.

³ "O, how fulfilled are those who recognize their own poverty of spirit because they shall enter the Spirit dimension.

⁴ "O, how fulfilled are those who let themselves feel the full intensity of their pain because they will ultimately experience complete joy.

⁵ "O, how fulfilled are those who have all their instincts under control because they will be in harmony with all of nature.

⁶ "O, how fulfilled are those who hunger for right relations in all things because they will find them.

⁷ "O, how fulfilled are those who can forgive other people because God will forgive them.

⁸ "O, how fulfilled are those who know who they are and what they are to do because they will experience God in the depths of their being.

⁹ "O, how fulfilled are those who create unity and harmony between others because they will be identified as God's offspring.

¹⁰ "O, how fulfilled are those who endure pain and persecution for their part in the God movement because they will enter the Spirit dimension.

¹¹ "Each of you will be fulfilled despite the verbal incriminations or physical attacks made upon you. ¹² Celebrate your participation in the God movement now and the participation you have in the final triumph which also is yours.

¹³ "You are the seasoning of the world, but if the seasoning loses its taste, it is good for nothing but to be cast into the garbage.

¹⁴ "You are a flashing light in the flow of history, showing it the way. A large beacon that is set on a hill cannot be hidden. ¹⁵ No person lights a lamp and covers it with a black cloth, but rather holds it in his hand so that he can shine it on the pathway in order that others can see the way to go. ¹⁶ Let your own actions light the way of other persons so that they may discover the way to live and, knowing that the source of your being is in God, they will fulfill his purpose and plan and thank him in the process.

Jesus points beyond the Law

¹⁷ "Do not interpret my ministry and message as wiping out your law—not anything which has been recorded. I have not come to destroy the past, but rather to fulfill that which was always present in it. ¹⁸ I tell you the truth, until the ultimate consummation of history, not one part of your past (not a word or even a letter) will be abolished until all of its potential is actualized.

¹⁹ "If anyone, therefore, tries to abolish these rules and if he teaches others to do the same, he will have a minor place in the Spirit dimension; but those who recognize their true intent and share their insight with others, these shall participate more fully. ²⁰ I tell you this, though, unless your relationships flow from the heart and not from the head (as do those of the interpreters of the rules and the pious Rulekeepers), you will not participate in the Spirit dimension.

²¹ "In the past, your teachers have said, 'You shall not kill and if anyone kills, he will have to face the consequences of his action.' ²² But I tell you, 'If anyone is unjustifiably angry with another person, he will have to face the consequences of his feelings; if anyone calls another person bad names, he will have to give an account of his behavior in the court. And if anyone completely discounts another person, he is in danger of losing his own personhood.

²³ "So if you are ever praying or offering your gifts to God in worship and at that time recall one of your fellow human beings who has a case against you—²⁴ drop your praying, stop your worship, go find your brother or sister and make peace, *then* come and offer your prayer and your worship. ²⁵ Develop the habit of agreeing with those persons who antagonize and oppose you when it does not cost you your integrity. To foster arguments will result in lawsuits, courtroom trials, and even jail. ²⁶ Such a procedure is costly to both person and purse.

²⁷ "Your teachers years ago said, 'Do not commit adultery.' ²⁸ I tell you that adultery is more than an act; whoever in his mind pictures having sex with a person has already committed adultery in his inner being.

²⁹ "Let me make some comparisons between physical values and spiritual values. If your right eye sees things in such a way that it blocks your spiritual growth, pull your eye out of its socket and throw it away, for it is more desirable that one member of your body be lost than you lose the whole purpose and meaning of your life. ³⁰ Or if your right hand behaves in such a way that it blocks your spiritual growth, cut your hand off and throw it away, for it is more desirable that you lose one of your members rather than lose the whole purpose and meaning of your life.

³¹ "You also recall that your teachers of old said, "If anyone wearies of living with his wife, all he need do is formally dismiss her and that absolves him of all responsibility for her future welfare.' ³² I say to you, 'Whoever dismisses his wife without evidence that the relationship is already broken and dead causes her to commit adultery. Whoever marries one who is so divorced also commits adultery.'

³³ "Your teachers of old have also said, 'Do not swear falsely, but perform to the Lord what you have sworn to do.' ³⁴ I say to you, 'Don't swear.' Don't swear in heaven's name, for that really refers to God. ³⁵ Don't swear by the power and

meaning of the earth, for God is in that, too. Don't swear by holy places, for they, too, belong to God. [36] Don't swear by your own integrity because you can't change your essential being. [37] You are persons of integrity. Simply say yes or no. To amplify that statement any further by swearing in the name of heaven, of God, of the earth, of a holy place, or yourself is an acknowledgment that you are not quite clear with yourself.

[38] "Your teachers a long time ago said, 'Avenge evil; take an eye in place of an eye, or a tooth in place of a tooth if yours is destroyed.' [39] But I tell you, 'Don't fight back.' If a person slaps you on your right cheek, turn to him the left cheek also. [40] If someone files a suit against you, and would take away your coat, give him your overcoat as well. [41] And if a stranger asks you to walk with him one mile, be willing to walk with him two. [42] Give assistance to the person who asks for your help. For example, if a person seeks to make a loan, try to accommodate him.

[43] "The teachers of old said, 'Love your neighbor and hate your enemy.' [44] I say to you, 'Love your enemies, affirm those who discount you, be kind to those who fear you, and ask God to enlighten the manipulators and the profiteers.' [45] I ask you to function like this in your lives so that you may be a reflection of the mind and spirit of God who makes the sun light the paths of both the perverse and those who rightly relate themselves to life; and he causes it to rain on everyone's land, whether they worship him or not.

[46] "What value is it if you love those persons who love you and are kind to those persons who are kind to you? Even the notoriously evil persons in your society can return kindness for kindness. [47] If you recognize and honor only those with whom you are intimate, what is the difference between you and other people? Do not even those who have no awareness of God do that? [48] My final admonition to you is to be fully man as God is fully God.

Inward motivation vs. outward acts

6 ¹ "Now let me talk with you about the inwardness of a person's relation to God. Regarding your contributions to worthwhile causes, do not stage your giving so that you will get attention from others, because if you do, you may escape your heavenly Father's attention. ² When you make your contribution, don't go hire a marching band to get the world's attention as the great religious pretenders do. When they get the world's applause, that is all they can expect from their giving. ³ When you give to worthy causes, keep it a secret even from yourself; don't tell your neighbor and don't keep replaying your act of giving in your head. ⁴ Let your gift remain anonymous. You may be sure that your heavenly Father is aware of your generosity, and he will fulfill you with the gift of himself.

⁵ "Like giving, prayer is also a personal experience. When you offer your prayer, don't seek some place of public display like the church or athletic contests or political conventions or inaugural speeches. Those who pray there have their recognition from the crowds who hear them. ⁶ When you pray, withdraw into your inner being where you are alone with God. Let your prayers happen there, and the life you live will clearly demonstrate what happened in your encounter with God.

⁷ "Also when you offer prayers, there is no reason to be wordy like the uninstructed. Prayer is not just words, but also attitudes and awarenesses, so a lot of words do not mean a lot of prayer. ⁸ I emphasize to you that God is aware of you before you are aware of him, and he knows what you need before you utter a single word.

God seeks your inner self

⁹ "Here is a simple way for you to pray. 'Father, you are the heart of heaven. We reverence your name. ¹⁰ May the

movement of your being continue to its Ultimate Fulfillment. May your purpose be actualized on this earth. May it be demonstrated in our lives as completely as it is in heaven. [11] Enable us to get the physical necessities for our lives today. [12] Continually forgive our failures even as we forgive the failures of others. [13] Lead us by your hand. Do not test us. Liberate us from destructive structures and persons. I pray all of these things because yours is the power, the authority, and the fulfillment in all things, in all ways.'

[14] "But when you understand and accept other persons' failures, it is not nearly so difficult for you to believe that your Father understands and accepts you. [15] If you cannot understand and accept other persons' failures, how can you believe that your Father will understand and accept you?

[16] "Let me now point out to you the spiritual meaning of abstaining from food. When you decide to abstain from food for a period of time, do not act like the great religious pretenders, who neither wash their faces nor comb their hair. They march about with a sad expression on their faces so that it will be obvious to other people they are abstaining from food. Truly, I tell you, they have all the fulfillment they will get.

[17] "When, for spiritual reasons, you decide to abstain from food, then wash your face and comb your hair [18] so that your friends and acquaintances will be unaware of your inward decision. But during these times, present yourself to your Father in the inner depths of your being. There your Father will see your true motivation, and he will reveal himself to you in your life.

Fulfillment found in the Spirit dimension

[19] "I suggest to you that you do not seek your security in the accumulation of possessions. The treasures of this world are subject to corruption and decay; if their values increase sufficiently, someone will find a way to take them away from

you. ²⁰ I do suggest that you accumulate wealth for yourself in the spiritual dimension of life. In that dimension, there is no corruption nor decay; neither is there deceit and deprivation. ²¹ Wherever you place your highest values, you will be motivated to propel your life in that direction. (Valuing and motivation go together.)

²² "Remember how your eye sees for your body. If your eye is in clear focus, then your body will have good, clear direction. ²³ But if your eye is diseased and out of focus, your vision will be impaired and you will completely lose your sense of direction. Now if the inner light of your being goes out, you will be in the dark concerning the meaning and direction of your life—and how great will that darkness be!

²⁴ "No person can live with loyalty to conflicting values. That would be self-destructive schizophrenia. When a person finds himself in a conflicting situation, he must choose one and reject the other; he must devote himself to one to the neglect of the other. You simply cannot live with double loyalty—one to God and the other to material things.

²⁵ "When you have asked your father to help you obtain the physical necessities of life, do not be filled with anxiety about what you will eat or drink or wear. Remember, life is more than food and clothes. ²⁶ Let me illustrate. You see birds flying in the sky; they neither sow seed, reap harvests, nor store grain, and your Father sees that they have enough to eat.

"Now compare yourself with birds. ²⁷ If you should wish to change the gifts of nature with which you have been endowed, just how much do you suppose you could change your being? ²⁸ Consider the anxiety that you often feel about the clothes you have. Just look at your flowers growing in the yard. They spring up and grow and bloom. They don't work at growing and making themselves beautiful. ²⁹ Didn't I tell you that our wealthiest king, Solomon, was not clothed as elegantly as one of those blooming flowers in your yard? ³⁰ If God wishes to color the world with beautiful flowers, which are here today

[27

and gone tomorrow, do you not think he will put clothes on you?

³¹ "Again, I repeat, do not live with anxiety; don't keep asking 'What shall we eat? What shall we drink? Where will we get our clothes?' ³² All this continuous quest for more and more of the physical necessities occupies the full attention of those who are unaware of God's presence. I assure you that your Father, the source of your being, is aware of all your physical needs.

³³ "You are to give first priority to the Spirit dimension and to setting all your relationships right. When you get a proper perspective, these other things will take care of themselves. ³⁴ So I tell you, live in the here and now. Don't worry at all about tomorrow. Live tomorrow when it gets here; deal with its challenges and opportunities as they present themselves.

Don't evaluate other people

7 ¹ "Do not spend your time deciding whether people are good or bad, and then you will not be afraid that they or God are deciding whether you are good or bad. ² Whatever standard you use to evaluate other persons, you will use the same standard to evaluate yourself. And with whatever limited knowledge you measure out their punishment, you will measure out your own.

³ "In the process of evaluating another person, why do you see a speck in a brother's eye while you are oblivious to the two-by-four in your own? ⁴ I must say, it is quite presumptuous for you to offer to wipe a speck out of his eye when you may jab his good eye with the two-by-four in your own. ⁵ O pretender, take the two-by-four out of your eye so that you will not injure your brother when you are wiping the speck out of his. (Maybe when you suffer the pain of removing the two-by-four, you may be willing for your brother to wipe his own eye.)

⁶ "Do not expose the deepest values and motives of your

life to persons who cannot appreciate them, and don't talk with them about things that are most meaningful to you. Such vulnerability will probably permit them to cause you pain and suffering.

Guidelines for your life

7 "Here are three simple directives for living in the Spirit dimension: Ask for what you want, and you will get it; seek for what you need, and you will find it; knock on doors of opportunity, and they will open to you. 8 I repeat. Everyone who asks for what he wants gets it; and everyone who seeks for what he needs finds it; and everyone who knocks on the door of opportunity has it opened. 9 You who are fathers, listen to me. If your son should ask you for a piece of bread, would you give him a rock? 10 Or if he should ask you for a piece of meat, would you give him a live snake? 11 If you, then, being human respond to the legitimate desires and needs of your children, do you not know that to a greater extent, your Father, the source of all being, will give you the true needs and desires of your life?

12 "Here's an axiom by which to live: whatever you would like for yourself, grant that to every other person. When you treat others with this love, trust, and respect, you fulfill everything that the rules laid out and that the ancient spokespersons of God talked about. 13 Choose God's way and give it priority in your life because there are many easy choices you can make which will lead to meaninglessness and despair, and many persons will choose those routes. 14 Because the choice to express the Spirit dimension requires you to focus your life and bring it under control, few people will choose it. They would rather keep all their options open, a course which results in the loss of life and meaning.

15 "Look out for pious religious pretenders who appear to be sensitive and sincere, but inwardly are motivated by greed and the lust for power. 16 You will recognize the source of their

motivation by their behavior. You know that you don't gather grapes from blackberry vines, nor figs from cactus. [17] It takes a strong, healthy tree to produce good, edible fruit. And a blighted tree produces shriveled fruit. [18] A healthy tree will not produce blighted fruit, nor will a blighted tree produce edible fruit. [19] When you have a tree that does not produce good fruit, you cut it down and burn it up. (What are you going to do with these pious religious leaders whose behavior is evil?) [20] I have given you all of these illustrations about trees and fruit to illustrate that a person's behavior indicates the quality of his motivation.

Belief incomplete without congruent behavior

[21] "While I am speaking about behavior and motivation, let me say that not every person who says the religious words, 'Lord, Lord,' will enter into the Spirit dimension; rather, it is the person whose behavior is congruent with God's intention who will enter the Spirit dimension. [22] On the day of the Ultimate Fulfillment of history, many participants in the building of that history will say the religious words, 'Lord, Lord,' and they will even say, 'We have preached, we have healed split personalities, we have done many good things.' [23] But I will have to say to them, 'Regardless of your words and your benevolent actions, you never really participated in the Spirit dimension. Get away from me. You have actually done evil rather than good.'

[24] "With this presentation I have summarized my teaching about the Spirit dimension. If you can hear what I am saying to you and shape your life according to the principles which I have laid down, you will be like a wise person who built his house upon a firm foundation. [25] And all the elements in nature tried to destroy that house: it rained, it flooded, the winds blew, the trees fell, but the house stood firm because it had a solid foundation. [26] And those of you who are hearing the sound of my words, but making no decision about your be-

havior, will be like a foolish person who erected his house on sand. ²⁷ When the rain and wind and floods came, that house collapsed, and its destruction was a tragedy."

²⁸ When Jesus had outlined these principles to the crowd, they were astonished. They found it difficult to accept his teaching. ²⁹ And yet, he instructed the people as one having his own authority, not as the interpreters of the rules who depended upon the authority of others.

Jesus heals

8 ¹ When Jesus had concluded his teaching, he came down the mountain accompanied by large crowds. ² On the way to his headquarters, he was met by a leper who bowed to him in reverence and said with great faith, "Sir, if you choose, you can make me whole." ³ Contrary to common practice, Jesus touched the leper with his hand, saying, "I want you to become whole." At once, the leprosy disappeared. ⁴ Looking deeply into the man's eyes, Jesus instructed him, "Do not tell a single person what I have done; rather, present yourself to the religious leaders and make the kind of contribution which is prescribed in the rules. Let both your gift and your presence witness to them."

⁵ As he entered Capernaum, where he had made his headquarters, a Roman army officer came to him with an urgent request. ⁶ "Sir, I have a servant at my house who is paralyzed, and he is suffering beyond description." ⁷ "Then I will come and make him whole," replied Jesus. ⁸ Anxiously the soldier spoke up again—"Sir, even with my station and rank, I don't deserve your coming to my house, but if you will just say the word, I believe that my servant will be made whole. ⁹ You see, like yourself, I am a man with authority. I have soldiers under me and I say to this one, 'Go!' and he does it, and to another one, 'Come!' and he comes, and to a servant in my household, 'Do this!' and he does it."

¹⁰ The official's response so amazed Jesus, that he turned to

the crowd following him and said, "I tell you the truth, I have not experienced this depth of faith before, not even in the chosen people who presumably have faith. [11] Because these chosen people do not demonstrate genuine faith, there will come a time when other persons will be gathered together from the East and the West, and they will fellowship in the Spirit dimension with Abraham, Isaac, and Jacob. [12] But those who originally were destined for the Spirit dimension will be left with no purpose and direction, and the pain of their existence will be unbearable."

[13] After issuing this brief rebuke to the chosen people, Jesus then turned to the soldier and said, "Go on home because what you have believed is really true, and it will happen just as you have said." From the time Jesus made that declaration, the official's servant was healed.

[14] Later Jesus went to Peter's house and found his mother-in-law suffering with a high fever. [15] When he touched her body with his hand, her fever was cured. Immediately she felt better, got up, and served them a meal.

[16] Another day, though it was sundown, the people continued to bring to Jesus those who were split in their persons, and just by speaking a word, he reunited them with themselves, and, in addition, he healed all who were sick. [17] These acts of healing were predicted by Isaiah, when he said, "He will take our pains and bear our sickness in his own body."

[18] One day when Jesus wearied from dealing with the large crowds that were all about him, pushing him, desiring to touch him, he told his followers to get into a boat and go over to the other side of the lake. [19] As they were leaving, one of the interpreters of the rules said, "Teacher, I will go with you anywhere." [20] To this one would-be follower Jesus stated, "The foxes have their dens and the birds their nests, but the Representative Man does not own a house."

[21] About that time another would-be follower said, "Sir, permit me to go home for my father's funeral, and then I will

accompany you." ²² To him, Jesus responded, "Accompany me now. Let those who are dead spiritually take care of burying those who are dead physically."

Jesus uses his extraordinary powers

²³ With these parting remarks, Jesus got into the boat with his followers. ²⁴ While they were crossing the lake, they encountered a sudden windstorm. It was so intense that their boat was covered with waves. Being weary from his day's work, Jesus had fallen asleep. ²⁵ While the storm was raging, his followers shook him awake and cried, "Lord, take care of us! We will be killed!" ²⁶ "Why are you full of fear, you of little trust?" Jesus responded. With the boat reeling, Jesus stood up and spoke to the wind and the sea. Both settled down and there was calm. ²⁷ Those who were with him were overwhelmed and murmured among themselves, "Who is this man who heals sick minds and bodies and also has authority over the elements of nature?"

²⁸ After that interlude with the wind and the waves, they came to the other side of the lake, to the region of the Gadarenes. As they were getting out of the boat, two raging schizoids came out of the caves up on the hillside, their abnormal behavior discouraging anyone's going along the pathway. ²⁹ Both of them screamed out of their separated selves, "Why have you come to confront us, Jesus, Son of God? It is not yet time for the confrontation. Are you here to punish us?"

³⁰ Several hundred yards away, there was a herd of pigs rooting and eating. ³¹ So those split parts pleaded with Jesus, saying, "If you plan to unite these men with themselves, don't let us float away in the air; rather, permit us to inhabit that herd of pigs." ³² Jesus said, "Take your leave." The divisive force which had tormented the men suddenly inhabited the herd of pigs, creating such consternation that the whole herd dashed headlong down the slope into the lake and drowned. ³³ Those who had been guarding the pigs ran into the city to

tell the story of their destruction and the subsequent healing of the two men. ³⁴ On hearing the report, the whole city came out to meet Jesus. When they came within earshot, they yelled at him and demanded that he leave their part of the country.

Jesus makes body and spirit whole

9 ¹ After this encounter, Jesus got back into the boat, crossed the lake, and went to Capernaum where he had headquartered the Spirit movement. ² As he arrived home, several neighbors brought to him a paralyzed man lying on a mat. Seeing the confidence of his friends, Jesus said to the paralyzed man, "Celebrate, my brother, because all of your misdoings are forgiven."

³ When several interpreters of the rules heard what he said, they immediately thought, "This man is saying that he is God." ⁴ Their facial and bodily expressions reflected to Jesus what was going on inside them. He questioned, "Why do you make false assumptions about my actions? ⁵ Do you consider that I am placing myself in God's role when I make a man whole spiritually more than when I make him whole physically?"

⁶ In order that these observers could understand that this Representative Man had authority from God to wipe out wrongdoing, he said to the paralyzed man, "You are also physically whole. Get up, pick up your mat, and go home to your family." ⁷ And the man got up and went to his home. ⁸ When the crowd witnessed that incident, they were aghast. In the grip of amazement, they offered thanks to God for delegating such authority to a man.

Calling the fragmented

⁹ After Jesus had made the paralyzed man both physically and spiritually whole, he left the headquarters and went down the street. He saw a man named Matthew sitting in his office collecting taxes. He said to him, "Come, associate yourself

with me." And Matthew got up and joined himself to Jesus.

¹⁰ As their relationship deepened, Matthew decided to give a dinner party in his home. Jesus was the guest of honor, and he was joined by a number of tax collectors and disreputable people, along with his understudies. ¹¹ During the meal, several of the pious Rulekeepers pulled the followers off to one side and asked, "Why is your teacher dining with these tax collectors and disreputable persons?"

¹² Jesus overheard their questioning and confronted them directly: "Those who are healthy don't need a doctor; only those who are sick need his attention. ¹³ I really don't think you understand what that means because you consider yourselves already healthy and whole. Listen again to what I have been emphasizing to you pious Rulekeepers: 'I prefer the purity of your deepest motivation more than all your external performances.' " Jesus continued, "I am not here to invite the whole into wholeness, but rather those who are fragmented and fractured."

New life, not new rules

¹⁴ Sometime after that dinner party, several of John the Baptizer's followers came to Jesus. They asked him, "Why is it that we have been taught, along with the pious Rulekeepers, to abstain from food, but your followers don't abstain at all?"

¹⁵ Jesus answered, "Do you think guests at a wedding will be in mourning while the bridegroom is present? However, later on, when the bridegroom leaves them, they will then abstain from food. ¹⁶ This religious practice of abstaining from food may not fit into the new order of life as it has in the old. You see, a tailor does not sew an unshrunk piece of cloth onto a garment that he has already shrunk. Should he make that mistake, the new piece of cloth will shrink when the garment is washed and the tear will be greater than before. ¹⁷ Or, consider this analogy—when you make wine, you do not put new wine into old wineskins that have already stretched to their

limit, because when the new wine ferments, it will burst the wineskins and be wasted. But you put new wine into new wineskins, and both are preserved. So I hope you understand that what I am teaching is a completely new way of living, not just a new set of religious practices."

Jesus continues healing

[18] While he was explaining this concept to John's followers, one of the Jewish officials came to him and with deep respect said, "Sir, my little girl is dead, but I believe that if you will come and touch her, she will come back to life." [19] Jesus, accompanied by his followers, got up and went with him.

[20] While they were on the way to the house of the official, a woman who had had a menstrual difficulty for more than a dozen years elbowed her way through the crowd and, summoning all her energy, lunged forward and touched just the hem of his robe. [21] She had already reasoned within herself, "If I can just touch the garment he is wearing, I will become whole." [22] The instant she touched his robe, Jesus stopped, turned around, and looked at her tenderly. He said, "My daughter, take heart! Your attitude of trust and expectancy has already made you a whole person." And it was true. This woman stopped bleeding from that very moment.

[23] When they arrived at the official's house, Jesus saw the professional mourners and the neighbors clamoring and carrying on. [24] He said, "Wait a minute—this little girl is not dead. She is only asleep." With that, they burst into laughter and ridicule. [25] However, when Jesus had stopped the noise and gone into the official's house, he took the girl by the hand and she got up. [26] The report of his bringing to life this official's daughter spread throughout the whole countryside.

[27] When Jesus left the house of the Jewish official and started back to his headquarters, his attention was directed to two blind men calling aloud to him, "David's son, help us!

Help us!" [28] They followed him all the way to his home, even into the house. Jesus said to them, "Is it your belief that I can cause you to see?" "Oh, yes!" they declared. [29] He then touched their eyes with the tips of his fingers, saying, "What you have believed in the depths of your being will be true in your body." [30] Their eyes were healed and they could see again. Immediately Jesus carefully instructed them, "Don't tell anyone what I have done. I don't want anyone to know about it." [31] Quite to the contrary, when they left his house, they told their experience to everyone they met, and Jesus' reputation spread throughout the countryside.

[32] As soon as these two men left, a man was brought to him who was unable to utter a single word. He had not always been that way, but had had an experience that left him speechless. [33] When Jesus removed his speech impediment, the man immediately began to talk. The crowd again was gripped with amazement, saying, "Our nation has never seen such activity before." [34] But the Rulekeepers, quite unwilling to believe that God was acting in this man Jesus, said, "He gets rid of these infirmities with power from the ruler of destruction."

Workers needed

[35] Unaffected by their evaluation, Jesus continued to travel through the towns and villages explaining his message in their meetings, and demonstrating the good news of the Spirit dimension by making people both physically and spiritually whole. [36] In his journeys, each time he saw the crowds gather, he was moved in the depths of his being with caring and concern because so many of them lived aimless and purposeless lives. [37] On such occasions he confided to his understudies, "The task ahead of us is momentous, and the workers to get it done are so few. [38] Pray that the Creator of life will multiply workers in the world, so that those who live meaningless lives will be restored to wholeness and hope."

The understudies are commissioned

10 ¹ On one occasion, Jesus assembled his twelve understudies and affirmed to them their authority to make persons whole—their authority prevailed over destructive forces that divided men and women within themselves, as well as over diseases which made them sick. ² Here's a list of the twelve understudies whom he appointed: Simon, whom he called Peter; and Andrew, his brother; then there were James and John, the sons of Zebedee; ³ Philip and Bartholomew; Thomas and Matthew, who was a tax collector; James, the son of Alphaeus, and Thaddaeus; ⁴ Simon the revolutionary; and Judas Iscariot, who eventually handed Jesus over to his enemies.

⁵ These twelve men Jesus commissioned and sent forth to share in his ministry. In preparation for their departure he said, "Don't go to the non-Jews at this time, and neither spend time with the half-Jews. ⁶ Give priority to the Jews who have lost their awareness of the God whom you are going out to proclaim. ⁷ As you go through the countryside, say to all the people, 'The breaking in of the Spirit dimension is imminent.' ⁸ In your encounters, make people whole. Give health to the sick, cleanliness and acceptance to lepers, life to the dead, and unity to persons who are divided within themselves. You have gotten your message from me without any cost, so give it to others without any charge.

⁹ "Don't bother to take any money or valuables with you. ¹⁰ Don't take anything to pay your own way. Don't even take a change of clothing or an extra pair of shoes; neither do I want you to take anything with which to protect yourselves. The person who shares himself and the message of God's claim on the world deserves to have his physical necessities provided for him.

¹¹ "When you enter a city, ask around until you discover the person who will be most receptive to your message, then offer

to stay with him as long as you are in that particular city.
¹² And when you approach the man's house whom you have
chosen, give him your positive reasons for choosing his house.
¹³ If the man does receive you and proves as receptive as his
reputation has indicated, give your blessing to him and his
household. If he does not respond to you, don't worry about
that; your blessing will return to you.

¹⁴ "While you are abiding in this man's house, preach and
teach as I have taught you; and if you find that some do not
receive your message, do not let that be an obstacle to you.
When you leave that house, leave with them the responsibility
for their choices, and don't burden yourself with a sense of
responsibility for their decision. ¹⁵ I tell you the truth, the fate
of those ancient cities of Sodom and Gomorrah will seem
mild compared to what happens to those cities which reject
you.

Jesus cautions his understudies

¹⁶ "Let me forewarn you about some of the experiences you
will encounter on your journey. I am asking you to be as
nonresistant to evil as sheep are to vicious wolves; be as wily
as a snake and as innocent as a dove. ¹⁷ Be wary of the persons who listen to you. Hidden in the crowd, there will be
persons who will take you to court, and others who will beat
you up even in the religious meeting houses. ¹⁸ In the course
of your mission, you can expect to be brought before the governing authorities because of the witness which you are making before them on my behalf.

¹⁹ "When you are apprehended and dragged into court, don't
worry in advance about what you will say. When it is neces-
sary for you to bear witness, you will receive sudden inspiration at that very moment concerning what you are to say. ²⁰ Be
confident that when you speak it is not some tale you have
contrived, but the Spirit of God, your Father, who speaks
through you.

²¹ "Not only will vicious men try to destroy you, but because of your message, whole families will be divided: brothers will oppose brothers, parents will oppose their children, and children will oppose their parents, even causing them to be executed. ²² And persons from all walks of life, from all the communities you visit will despise you because you preach my message and participate in my mission. But the person who perseveres to the completion of the age will find personal wholeness and fulfillment.

²³ "When the resistance becomes too great in one city, go to another. You will have not covered all of the cities in this nation till the Representative Man makes his appearance. Expect that. ²⁴ Keep in mind that the student is not above the teacher, nor the employee above the employer. ²⁵ It is enough to expect the student will become as the teacher and the employee as the employer. Now consider a specific application of that insight. If our opponents have called the head of the house 'the prince of devils,' what do you suppose they will say about his children? ²⁶ Regardless of what they say, don't be afraid. One day the truth will be known by all, and at that time your true motives as well as those of your opponents will be exposed for everyone to see. ²⁷ What I have shared with you in the long nights of training, proclaim courageously in broad, open daylight. What I have whispered in your ear, shout on the street corners of the city.

²⁸ "Again I say to you, don't be afraid of those who can destroy your body, but have no power to touch your spirit. Rather, reverence the one who is the source of both your spirit and your body. ²⁹ Stay in touch with your personal worth. You are aware that you can buy a couple of sparrows for a penny. Don't you know that not one of those can fall wounded to the earth without your Father being aware of it? ³⁰ He is aware of everything about you, even how many hairs you have on your head. ³¹ Do not be anxious for your safety,

because persons are much more valuable than a sparrow. ³² Remember that whoever speaks my name and my message before other persons, I will confess his name and his faithfulness before my Father who is in heaven. ³³ Conversely, whoever repudiates my message before other persons I will repudiate before my Father who is in heaven.

Seek complete relationship with God

³⁴ "Don't be captured by the illusion that our mission will always create unity on the earth. In some instances, it will actually create division rather than unity. ³⁵ I am aware that my ministry will cause a man to oppose his father and a daughter to oppose her mother and a daughter-in-law to oppose her mother-in-law. ³⁶ You will discover that a person's greatest opposition will often be from his/her own family. ³⁷ But remember that a person who loves father or mother more than me cannot have a complete relationship with me. And a parent who loves his son or daughter more than me cannot have a complete relationship with me. ³⁸ Anyone who does not take his commitment to me with utmost seriousness, even to giving his life for me, cannot have a complete relationship with me. ³⁹ The person who finds this complete relationship with me will discover real life, and his unproductive relationships will fall away. The person who loses these old relationships because he is related to me will certainly find a real life.

⁴⁰ "Because you are related to me, everyone who relates to you relates to me, and everyone who relates to me relates to the one who sent me. ⁴¹ The person who respects the spokesman of God and relates to him as such will participate in that spokesman's reward. In like manner, the person who appreciates the value of another person's relationship and respects him for his life style will participate in the benefits of it. ⁴² Let me apply these principles in the simplest way to the

task you are undertaking. Whoever recognizes you and gives you a drink of water because you are an understudy of mine, I tell you truthfully that person will participate in the benefits of the relationship which you have with me."

About John the Baptizer

11 ¹ After Jesus had concluded his instructions to his twelve understudies, he himself left the headquarters to join them in teaching and preaching in the nearby cities. ² When John the Baptizer, who now was in jail, heard reports of the marvelous activities of the Christ, he began to feel the need for personal reassurance. ³ So he sent two of his understudies to Jesus with this question: "Are you the person we have expected to come all through the ages, or must we still wait and look for him later?"

⁴ Rather than give a direct "yes" or "no" answer, Jesus said to John's followers, "Report to John once again the things which you yourself have heard and witnessed; namely, ⁵ blind persons are seeing, lame persons are walking, leprous persons are made whole, deaf persons are hearing, dead persons are coming to life, and poor persons are hearing good news which liberates them. ⁶ Remind John that every person will be fulfilled who does not give up his trust in me."

⁷ When John's followers were out of earshot, Jesus turned to the crowd with him and spoke about John the Baptizer. "When you went out into the desert to hear what the Baptizer had to say, what did you expect? Did you expect a man who had bent to popular opinion like a reed responds to a stiff wind? ⁸ What did you expect? Did you expect to find a man dressed in stylish clothes—those stylish dressers are among the elite. ⁹ Again I ask, what did you expect to see in the desert? A person who would tell things as they are? Well, that is exactly what you found and even more than that. ¹⁰ For the spokesman you went to hear is the one written about in our ancient

scriptures: 'Take note, because I send my representative before you to prepare the way for you to walk in.' [11] I tell you the truth, there has never been a person born by the process of nature that is greater than John the Baptizer; still, the person who is born into the Spirit dimension has a greater awareness and perception than he does. [12] From the time John the Baptizer began his ministry, the Spirit dimension has been under attack, and those persons bound to rules and regulations have sought to force their way into it. [13] You see, until John made his appearance, the spokesmen of old and the lawgivers had spoken of the future. [14] If you can believe it, the Baptizer is really Elijah, whom you have expected to return and initiate a new era. [15] If you have ears, then listen to what I am saying.

[16] "I have searched for a symbol which would best express your actions and responses. You are like children sitting on the curb of the street yelling out to your playmates, [17] 'We have made music, but you won't dance with us; we have cried our eyes out, and you won't shed a tear.' [18] You see, John presented himself as an ascetic and you said, 'He is possessed by an alien spirit.' [19] The Representative Man came as a regular person eating and drinking with the people and you say, 'Look at that glutton, that wino; he is a bosom buddy of tax collectors and disreputable people.' Oh, well, I suppose that true wisdom can never be found in what a person does and doesn't do, if that's all the information you have about him."

Words of warning—and comfort

[20] After Jesus had pointed out to the people that they had rejected John's life style of an ascetic and that they also were rejecting his lifestyle as a real person enjoying life, he began to reprimand the persons in the cities who lived nearby because they had witnessed both his and John's actions and had neither changed their attitudes nor their actions. [21] "Be-

[43

ware, Chorazin! Beware, Bethsaida! If the ancient cities of Tyre and Sidon had witnessed the deeds which you have witnessed, they would have changed their attitude long ago and would have begun to show it in the lives which they lived. ²² Remember this. In the day of final reckoning, things will go easier for Tyre and Sidon than for you. ²³ A special word to you, Capernaum, in whose bosom I have made my headquarters. You have been exalted to the heights, but you will be brought down to the depths, for daily you have witnessed the power of God acting through me. I believe if the evil city of Sodom had seen all these deeds, it would have remained until this very day. ²⁴ Likewise, on the day of final reckoning, it will go easier for Sodom than for you."

²⁵ When Jesus had spoken these words, he seemed to be translated by the Spirit. He spoke this prayer: "My father, the source of everything that is in the universe, you have made it impossible for the rationalists and the moralists in their own strength to discover you, but you have revealed yourself to persons untutored in philosophy and ethics. ²⁶ Yes, Father, this was your way of showing people that they are dependent upon you. ²⁷ Father, you have placed everything in the universe under my authority and not a person on this earth knows me for who I really am; only you know me. But no person knows you either, except me and those to whom I reveal your nature."

²⁸ When he had concluded his prayer, he reached out his arms to the crowd around him and said, "Come into fellowship with me if you are tired and burdened, and I will refresh and release you. ²⁹ Take the burden of responsibility I give you and thereby discover your life and your destiny. I am gentle and humble; I am willing to relate to you and to permit you to learn at your own rate; then, in fellowship with me, you will discover the meaning of your life. ³⁰ My fellowship will release you, and my companionship will direct you on your journey."

Why should rules hinder good deeds?

12 ¹ On another occasion, Jesus and his understudies were cutting through a grain field on the Jewish day of rest. His understudies were hungry, so they began pulling heads of grain and eating them. ² Trailing along at a distance were several pious Rulekeepers. When they saw what his followers were doing, they began their accusation, "Look what your followers are doing! They are breaking the rules of our day of rest."

³ Jesus countered, "Don't you know your history? Don't you remember what David, your king, did and those who accompanied him? ⁴ You recall how he entered the place of worship and ate bread which was reserved for priests only. ⁵ Haven't you read your own modification of the rules? Your own religious leaders work in the temple on the day of rest, and they are held innocent. ⁶ I speak the truth to you. What I represent is of more significance than what the temple represents; thus, my understudies are as guiltless as David when he ate the bread, or your religious leaders when they break the rules. ⁷ I am sure you don't understand the principle to which I'm pointing. If you understood that the inner attitude of the heart is more important than the observance of external rules, you would not sit in judgment upon those who are innocent. ⁸ For your information, the Representative Man is in charge of all the rules, including the rules about the day of rest." ⁹ After this encounter with the Rulekeepers, Jesus went on to their meeting house.

¹⁰ As he and his understudies were going into the meeting house, they walked past a man whose hand was deformed. Again, Jesus was accosted by the pious Rulekeepers. "Is it all right to practice healing on the day of rest?" (They were looking for some infraction of the law so they could take him into court.)

¹¹ "Let me ask you a question," he proposed. "If one of your

[45

farmers has a sheep which falls into a pit on the day of rest, won't he grasp the sheep and pull it out of the pit? [12] If you're willing to assist a sheep, don't you think it would be more noble to assist a man? There are no rules against doing good on the day of rest."

[13] With that comment, Jesus said to the man whose hand was shriveled, "Extend your hand for me to see." As the man stretched forth his hand, it was restored to wholeness so that it looked just like the other one. [14] With that demonstration, the pious Rulekeepers went out, held a meeting, pronounced Jesus guilty, and started plotting his execution.

Ancient prophecy fulfilled

[15] Because Jesus was aware of their actions, he departed from that city. As he left, huge crowds followed him, and he continued to make many persons whole. [16] Each time he liberated some person from misery, he requested that individual not to tell anyone about it. [17] These mighty acts, which he continued to perform, fulfilled the prediction made by Isaiah, the spokesman of old. [18] He had said, "Observe my chosen representative, the one whom I love very dearly, the one with whom I am delighted. I have placed my spirit in him, and he will reveal the right thing to the non-Jews. [19] He will not fight, neither will he complain. No person will witness him crying in the streets. [20] He will not add to the oppression of anyone; neither will he intensify the suffering which they experience until the way that he represents prevails throughout the earth. [21] And all the non-Jews will put their faith in this Representative Man whom I have chosen."

[22] On another occasion a person was brought to him who was deeply divided within himself; he was also blind and speechless. Jesus united him within himself and enabled him to see and speak. [23] A sense of awe swept over the crowd when they saw what he did. They said, "Isn't this the son of David, the new king whom we have been expecting to deliver and rule us?"

God is not divided

²⁴ The mention of a new ruler threatened the Rulekeepers, and they made their attack: "This man has been given all this power by the ruler of the demonic." ²⁵ When Jesus heard their evaluation, he said, "Every nation which is divided against itself will be destroyed, and every city or household divided against itself will fall down. ²⁶ And if the ruler of the demonic dimension attacks the demonic, then that ruler of evil is divided against himself. How can the demonic dimension stand if it is so divided? ²⁷ If I make people whole by the power of the demonic, by what power do some of your representatives make people whole? (Are your healers also demonic?) ²⁸ On the other hand, if I overcome the demonic by the Spirit of God, then the Spirit dimension has been demonstrated to you.

²⁹ "But consider one more question. How can you break into a strong man's house and steal his valuables, except first you conquer the man? When you have conquered him, then you can take what you want from him. (Do you now understand the relationship which I have with the demonic?) ³⁰ Whoever is not cooperating with me in the conquest of the demonic opposes me. Whoever does not work with me toward unity, wholeness, and fulfillment is creating division and destruction. ³¹ I tell you that persons can have all kinds of failure forgiven, even experiences of making holy things common, except they will not be forgiven for making the Holy Spirit common. ³² For example, if anyone accuses the Representative Man of evil, that can be forgiven. But if anyone continually opposes the Holy Spirit, that opposition cannot be forgiven in this era nor in the one coming.

You are accountable

³³ "Either get your life in union with God and let your behavior demonstrate that, or else let your life get completely out of control and your behavior will reflect that. A person's

inner life is recognized by his behavior. [34] So many of you listening to me are self-deluded pretenders. When you are out of union with God, how can you talk about what is good? Don't you realize that the words which come out of your mouth express your innermost being? [35] If a person's behavior is good, it is because he is drawing out of the inner life of union with God. If a person's behavior is destructive, it is likewise because he is acting from a distorted or confused relationship with God. [36] Truly, I tell you that every word which you speak is an indicator of your relationship with God, and for this you are accountable. [37] So what you say symbolizes how it is between you and God; your words either point toward wholeness or toward destruction."

Seek new life, not miracles

[38] The representative group from the interpreters of the rules and from the Rulekeepers said, "Teacher, show us some miracles." [39] Immediately he reacted, saying, "Only a group of persons who are cut off from their roots and have become fascinated with magic want to see a miracle. There is only one miracle that you will see, and it is that one which Jonah, the spokesman of old, symbolizes. [40] As this ancient spokesman spent three days and nights in a big fish, so the Representative Man will spend three days and three nights in the earth's stomach. [41] The citizens of that ancient city of Nineveh will reproach you on the day of reckoning because they changed their attitudes and lifestyle under the teaching of Jonah. And a more significant person than Jonah has spoken to you. [42] Also the pagan queen who came out of the South to Solomon will accuse you on that day of reckoning. She came a long way to hear Solomon's wisdom, yet I say to you a person greater than Solomon has spoken wisdom to you.

[43] "When a negative, unproductive way of life has been repressed, that old pattern is not abolished nor destroyed, but hangs around looking for a way to return and take over

48]

your life. ⁴⁴ One day that pattern which has such great strength says, 'I will return to that person where I lived for so long and see if he has replaced me with another way of life.' If a new style has not replaced the old unproductive one, a strange thing will happen. ⁴⁵ That old pattern will return with seven times the power it previously had and will be more destructive than it was originally. The final condition of that person is far worse than the former. And that's how it will be with a whole generation of persons who do not find their center in God."

God's family is inclusive

⁴⁶ While he was addressing a huge crowd, his mother and his brothers stood at the edge of the crowd waiting until he finished so that they could speak to him. ⁴⁷ As he was concluding his remarks, someone interrupted, "Look, your mother and brothers are standing out there wanting to talk with you." ⁴⁸ To which Jesus replied, "Who is my mother, who are my brothers?" ⁴⁹ Then he pointed to his followers and some of the people in the crowd and said, "Look at my mother. Look at my brothers and sisters! ⁵⁰ Whoever actualizes the will of my Father who is present to the depth of your being, that person is my brother and sister and mother."

Jesus' stories reveal much

13 ¹ One morning, Jesus went out of his house in Capernaum and walked over to the beach. ² When it began to be known that he was there, a large crowd gathered, so big that Jesus stepped into a boat, pushed out from the land, and sat down. The crowd swelled until it crowded the beach. ³ Using simple stories he expressed to them many aspects of the Spirit dimension.

"A farmer went out to plant," he began. ⁴ "As he planted seed, some fell at the end of the row where he made his

turns; the birds swooped down and gobbled up these seed.
⁵ Another portion of the seed fell on a thin layer of earth under
which there was a slab of stone. These seeds sprouted quickly
because they were not planted deep. ⁶ After the sun had shone
on them a few days, they withered ,because they had no deep
root. ⁷ Some of the seed also fell among thorns, and the thorns
grew faster than the good seed and choked them. ⁸ But some
of the seed fell on good earth and produced an abundant
harvest—some a hundred times the original planting, others
sixty and others thirty. ⁹ If you can hear, listen to what I am
saying."

¹⁰ When his followers got Jesus alone, they asked him,
"Why are you always talking in stories?" "Because you have
me to explain to you the mystery of the Spirit dimension," he
answered, ¹¹ but it must remain a mystery for those who are
not my followers. ¹² The person who's been given some will be
given more, so that he'll really wind up with more than he
needs. But the person who doesn't have anything will even
have to give that up. ¹³ I speak to this crowd in stories because
they see without seeing, hear without hearing, and reason
without understanding the meaning of my stories. ¹⁴ One of
God's spokesmen of old, Isaiah, described this kind of people:
'You hear, but you don't hear with understanding; you see,
but you don't see with accurate perception. ¹⁵ This people's
inner sensitivity has become numb and their inner awareness
has become vague. They don't see the true meaning of things
because if they should really see and truly hear and know
intuitively, they would be transformed and made whole.' "

¹⁶ Then turning to his followers he said, "You are finding
fulfillment because you see with an inner vision and you hear
with the ears of your heart. ¹⁷ I tell you honestly, many of
God's spokespersons of old and many who have had a right
relationship with him have wished to see what you see and have
not seen it, and hear what you have heard and have not heard
it.

[18] "Now let me explain the story of the seed. [19] When a person hears about the Spirit dimension and does not grasp the message, those very thoughts are expelled from his mind and heart. This is what I meant by the seed which fell on the turn row. [20] The seed which fell on thin earth are like the person who hears about the Spirit dimension and very quickly and joyously embraces it. [21] Because he grasps it in his conscious mind, but it never gets into his deep mind, its influence will not last. When he faces active opposition and rejection, his interest in the Spirit dimension will evaporate. [22] Those seed falling in the midst of weeds represent the person who hears about the Spirit dimension but has difficulty ordering his life according to spiritual values. Quite soon his earthly responsibilities or the illusion of security that wealth offers choke the inspiration of the Spirit dimension, and he goes on living a barren life. [23] But the good soil represents the person who hears about the Spirit dimension and understands it. He fashions his life accordingly and expresses the values of the Spirit dimension in his lifestyle, some a hundred times again, others sixty, and still others thirty."

Jesus describes the Spirit dimension

[24] He told them another story. "The Spirit dimension is like a farmer who planted good seed in his field. [25] While that farmer slept, an enemy of his went through his field sowing weeds among the good seed, and then went on his way. [26] When the good seed first sprouted and came up, they didn't look too different from the weeds. Later on, however, the weeds became apparent. [27] So one day, the farmhands said to their employer, 'Didn't you sow good seed in the fields? Where did these weeds come from?' [28] The farmer answered, 'An enemy of mine has done this.' The farmhands said, 'Do you want us to pull up the weeds?' [29] 'No,' said the farmer, 'while you are pulling up the weeds, you may also pull up the wheat and I would lose the whole crop. [30] Let the weeds and the wheat

grow together until harvest time. When we are harvesting, I will instruct those of you who do the reaping, 'Gather the weeds, bale them and burn them up, but store the wheat in the barn.' "

[31] Here's another story describing the Spirit dimension. "The growth of the Spirit dimension within a person can be compared to small grains of mustard seed. When a farmer plants one in his field, it is the smallest of all seeds. [32] But when this tiny mustard seed is full grown, it is the largest of herbs. It grows into a bush large enough for birds to make nests and roost in its branches."

[33] He spoke still another story to them. "The Spirit dimension is like a small package of yeast with which a woman mixed three cups of flour; and it yeasted all the flour."

[34] That day Jesus told all these stories to the crowd, and he didn't say anything to them which was not in story form. [35] Again, this mode of speaking had been forecast by one of God's servants long ago when he said, "I will speak to you in stories; I will articulate mysteries which have been hidden from the creation of the world."

[36] When he finished speaking, Jesus dismissed the crowd and walked back over to his house. On the way, his understudies said, "Will you explain to us the story about the weeds in the field?" [37] Jesus responded, "The one who planted the good seed is the Representative Man. [38] The field is the world, and the good seed are the persons already born into the Spirit dimension, but the weeds are those persons who have chosen another source for their lives. [39] The enemy that directs them is the Adversary. The harvest points to the climax of history, and those who do the gathering and separating are God's workers. [40] As those weeds are baled and burned in the fire, that's how it will be at the climax of history. [41] The Representative Man will commission his associates to separate out those persons who have not been open to the Spirit dimension and thus blocked its expansion and progress. [42] And the pain felt

by those who are separated will be like burning in a fire, and there will be much sorrow. ⁴³ After that, those who have a right relationship with God will glow like the luster of the sun in the presence of their Father. If you have ears, then listen to what I am saying.

⁴⁴ "The Spirit dimension can also be compared to a trunk of gold buried in a field. If a person should inadvertently discover that trunk, he would cover it up and eagerly sell everything which he possesses to buy the field in which the treasure is hidden.

⁴⁵ "The Spirit dimension is also like a jeweler seeking precious stones. ⁴⁶ When he finds one jewel he appraises for an enormous sum of money, he will liquidate all his other holdings to purchase it.

⁴⁷ "Also, the Spirit dimension can be compared to a large net which is dropped into a lake and gathers fish of all kinds. ⁴⁸ When that net is full, the fishermen draw it to shore and sit down, separating the fish which are worth keeping from those which are not. ⁴⁹ A similar separation will take place at the climax of history when God's messengers will separate the true participants in the Spirit dimension from the pretenders. ⁵⁰ And the sense of loss which those pretenders will experience will be unbearable."

⁵¹ Jesus then questioned his understudies. "Do you understand what I am talking about?" They all nodded, "Yes, yes, we do." ⁵² Then he said to them, "Every person who understands the principle of the Spirit dimension is like a homeowner who has both precious antiques and modern furnishings —he can always display something new."

Jesus unwelcome at home

⁵³ When Jesus had finished telling these stories, he headed home to Nazareth where he was reared. ⁵⁴ When he neared his destination, he began teaching in their meeting places, and his hearers were astounded at what he said. "Where does this man

whom we know get all these insights, and where does he get the power to do what he is doing? [55] He is the son of the carpenter Joseph, isn't he? Isn't he Mary's son? Don't we know his brothers James, Joseph, Simon, and Judas? [56] And what about his sisters, aren't they still living here? We know where he came from as well as his family. How can he be saying all these things?"

[57] The truth is, they were rather put off by both his words and his behavior. Jesus responded, "A spokesperson for God gets recognition and acceptance from almost everyone except his family and the persons with whom he was reared." [58] Because of their unfaith, he did few miracles in Nazareth.

The death of John the Baptizer

14 [1] It was about this time that Herod, the governor of the region, began hearing reports about the phenomenal activities of Jesus. [2] Out of his sense of guilt, he said to several of his associates, "This man is John the Baptizer. He has come back to life, and that's why these miraculous healings are taking place through him."

[3] Herod had arrested John and put him in jail at the insistence of Herodias, his wife, who was formerly married to his brother Philip. [4] On one occasion John had said to Herod, "It's wrong for you to be living with her." [5] He would have killed John at that moment, but he was afraid of the crowds since they considered John to be a spokesman for God. [6] When, however, Herod celebrated his birthday, Herodias' daughter performed an exotic dance which stimulated him greatly. [7] Without thinking, he offered her anything she wanted. [8] Directed by her mother, she said, "Present me with John the Baptizer's head on a platter."

[9] Her request grieved Herod, but he was faithful to his word and directed that her request be granted. [10] At his instructions, the soldiers beheaded John, who was in jail. [11] Then his head was placed on a platter and given to the young woman,

and she took it to her mother. [12] John's associates claimed his body and buried it, then went to tell Jesus what had happened.

Jesus feeds a multitude

[13] When Jesus heard about John's death, he crossed the lake and headed for the desert where he could find some solitude. News of his departure spread quickly, and a crowd collected around him. [14] Jesus approached the crowd, and as he looked into their eyes, he experienced a deep feeling of caring; those among the crowd who were sick, he touched and made whole.

[15] As the day wore on toward evening, his followers said to him, "We're out here in this desert and the day is mostly gone; dismiss the crowd so that they can go back to the villages and buy food." [16] But Jesus said, "They need not leave; you can give them something to eat." [17] His followers protested, "We don't have anything but five loaves of bread and two fish." [18] "Bring what you have to me," Jesus directed.

[19] Upon receiving it, he instructed the crowd to sit down on the grass. Then he took the bread and the fish and, in the presence of his Father, dedicated it. As he broke the food into pieces, he gave it to his followers, who passed it out to the crowd. [20] Everyone present had all that he or she needed to eat. When the meal was over, they picked up twelve sackfuls of leftovers. [21] That day the crowd numbered about five thousand males, besides the females and their children.

A lesson in faith for Peter

[22] As soon as they had gathered the leftovers, Jesus instructed his followers to get into a boat and to cross the lake while he dismissed the crowd. [23] As they started home at last, he went up to the hills for a time of solitude and prayer. By dark, he was there alone. [24] His followers in the boat had encountered an unexpected difficulty. A storm had arisen, and they were caught in the high winds and the choppy waves. [25] About three o'clock in the morning, Jesus made his way

toward them, walking on the surface of the lake. [26] When his followers saw him walking on the water, they were frightened and cried out, "Who is that? Is that a spirit?" [27] Jesus spoke to them at once and said, "Take it easy; it is I. You don't need to be afraid."

[28] Peter, being in doubt, responded, "Lord, if it really is you, then tell me to come to you walking on the water." [29] And he said, "Come on, then." Peter stepped over the side of the ship and began walking on the water toward Jesus. [30] When he realized how hard the wind was blowing, he became afraid and shouted, "Lord, rescue me!" as he began to sink.

[31] At once, Jesus held out his hand and caught him, then said, "Peter, you have shown such a small amount of trust; why did you begin to doubt?" [32] About the time Jesus and Peter got into the boat, the wind stopped blowing. [33] So overwhelmed were his understudies in the boat that they bowed in reverence, saying, "You must certainly be the Son of God."

[34] The boat landed on the other side of the lake in the region of Gennesaret. [35] When the people in that area knew that Jesus had arrived, they gathered up all of the sick and suffering people and brought them to him. [36] They requested that they might but touch the hem of his robe, and those who touched even his garment were made whole.

Jesus exposes the Rulekeepers

15 [1] Later on in Jesus' ministry, the Rulekeepers and the interpreters of the rules from Jerusalem approached him with this query: [2] "Why do your followers break the rules which our fathers made? You are aware that they eat their meals without going through the ceremonial cleansing." [3] Jesus answered them with a question, "Why do you disregard the directive from God by appealing to the rules which your fathers handed down to you? [4] God has said to you, 'Respect your father and your mother, and if any person disregards the needs of his parents, he must suffer the consequences of that choice.' ⁵ But you argue that if anyone says to his mother or father, 'All my resources are dedicated to God; whatever you should receive from me has already been given to God'—then he owes them nothing else. ⁶ By this maneuver, you refuse God's directive to respect the needs of your father and mother. In this way you have neutralized God's command by appealing to the rules of your culture. ⁷ You phonies! How accurately Isaiah described you when he said, ⁸ 'These people pretend to approach the center of my plan and purpose with their confessions and demonstrations, but their true motivation is quite different. ⁹ Their pretense at worship is empty, and the image of God and of reality to which they adhere arises out of human fantasy.' "

Let God control your basic motivation

¹⁰ When he finished that encounter, he beckoned the crowd to come closer. "I want you to listen to me and grasp what I am about to say. ¹¹ What a person eats or drinks does not make him unfit for God; rather, it is his basic motivation which indicates whether he is congruent with God's intention or not." ¹² One of his understudies spoke up, "Teacher, are you aware that the pious Rulekeepers felt put down by what you just said?" ¹³ Jesus answered, "Do you remember the stories of the plants in the field? Well, every plant which my Father has not planted will be pulled up. ¹⁴ Don't debate with the Rulekeepers. They are themselves insensitive to the plan and purpose of God, and they are guiding a group of persons who are insensitive to his plan and purpose. When insensitive people guide insensitive people, both wind up in meaninglessness and despair."

¹⁵ When he finished, Peter said to him, "Explain this story to us." ¹⁶ Jesus asked, "Are you also insensitive? ¹⁷ Surely you know that whatever a person eats or drinks goes into his stomach, is digested, and passes out through his bowels. ¹⁸ But a person's behavior arises out of his basic motivation,

and it is a person's basic motivation which determines whether he is fulfilling God's purpose and plan. [19] For example, out of the depths of a person's nature come evil fantasies, conflicting feelings, sexual unfaithfulness, sexual promiscuity, taking what belongs to another, telling what is untrue, and treating holy things as if they were commonplace. [20] These are the things that make a person unfit for God, not the neglect of rituals."

The Spirit dimension open to non-Jews

[21] After this explanation, Jesus left and went into the region around Tyre and Sidon. [22] There he was met by a woman from Canaan who came running up to him, crying out, "Be kind to me, Son of David. My daughter is so confused, so perplexed, so divided within herself." [23] Jesus was silent. One after another, his disciples tugged at his robe and said, "Tell her to go away; she's embarrassing us." [24] Jesus said to the woman, "My primary mission now, my daughter, is to the people of Israel who have lost their sense of direction." [25] Disregarding his explanation, she reverently knelt at his feet and pleaded, "Sir, help me." [26] Jesus declared, "If my Father's purpose for me now is to feed the Jewish people, it is not proper for me to take their bread and distribute it to the non-Jews." [27] "True, sir," she said, "but is it not also true that the non-Jews could gather up the Jews' leftover crumbs from under the table?" [28] Jesus was moved at her response and said, "Woman, you have a tremendous faith. You will get exactly what you want." And Jesus said that her daughter was well.

Jesus feeds another huge crowd

[29] After the encounter Jesus went over near the lake of Galilee, made his way up a mountain, and sat down. [30] Then great crowds thronged around him, bringing the crippled, the blind, the speechless, the deformed, all kinds of sick people, and placed them in front of him. And Jesus made them whole.

[31] When the huge crowds witnessed the mute speaking, the deformed made whole, the crippled walking, and the blind seeing, they offered thanks and praise to God.

[32] After Jesus had been healing and teaching for several days, he beckoned his understudies together around him. He said, "I am truly concerned about this crowd because they have been with me for three days and have had nothing to eat. I cannot send them away without food lest they grow faint on the way home." [33] His understudies were stunned by his statement. "Where can we get enough food out here in the desert to feed such a crowd?" [34] Jesus took inventory of their food. "How many loaves of bread do you have?" And they said, "Seven, and a few fish." [35] Then he stood up and directed the crowd to sit down in small groups on the ground. [36] Taking the seven loaves and the fish, he offered thanks to God and began distributing the food to his understudies, who passed it on to the crowd. [37] Everyone there had something to eat until each one was full. When they had finished eating, they gathered up seven sacks filled with leftovers. [38] That day the crowd numbered about four thousand males, besides the females and the children. [39] After the meal he dismissed the crowd and took a boat to the coast of Magadan.

Watching for signs

16 [1] Later on, the Rulekeepers and the religious aristocrats sent delegations to interview Jesus. They demanded, "Give us indisputable evidence of your identity and what you are up to." [2] In response Jesus said, "Late in the afternoon you survey the sky. If it appears to be red, you predict fair weather for the next day. [3] But when the sky is dark and threatening, you predict rain. You pretenders! You can read the message written in the sky, but you cannot read the meaning of the events that are happening right around you. [4] You are a blind and confused generation with divided loyalties, and no indisputable evidence will be given to you except that symbolized by God's spokesman Jonah."

Then Jesus turned around and walked away from them. [5] He and his followers got into a boat and sailed across the lake. When they got to the other side, they remembered that they had taken no food along. [6] Jesus turned to his followers, saying, "Take note of the yeast of these pious Rulekeepers and proud aristocrats." [7] The followers began to speak among themselves, "What's he talking about? Yeast? He uses symbols so often he must be referring to the fact that we didn't bring any bread along."

[8] When Jesus realized what they were talking about, he said, "You have so little trust in me and what I can do. [9] Don't you remember the day we fed five thousand persons with five loaves of bread? How many sacks of leftovers did you pick up that day? [10] Or don't you remember the seven loaves of bread with which we fed four thousand people? How many sacks of leftovers did you pick up that day? [11] Surely you understand that I am not talking about bread and your failure to bring some along for us to eat. I am speaking to you about the influential teaching of those two groups of leaders— those who are pious legalists and those who are skeptical aristocratic rulers."

[12] The followers got the point. They realized he was not talking about bread at all, but rather the influence that the ideas of the Rulekeepers and religious aristocrats could have on them.

Peter affirms the Messiah

[13] By this time, they had docked the boat on the beach in Caesarea Philippi. When they had sat down on the beach, Jesus said to his understudies, "When the crowds talk about me, who do they call the Representative Man?" [14] They replied, "They refer to you by various names. Some call you John the Baptizer; some Elijah, some Jeremiah, or others just say you're one of God's spokespersons." [15] Quite pointedly he asked, "Who do you think I am?" [16] Simon Peter answered,

"You are the Messiah, the unique representative of God who is alive and active among us." [17] Jesus affirmed, "You're experiencing the fulfillment, Simon, son of John; you did not arrive at that answer by logic or intuition. Only my Father could have given you that answer. [18] You are the Rock—and on the rock of your confession I will build a community of persons who are related to me. The combined forces of evil will not prevail over this community. [19] I will enable you to understand the principles of the Spirit dimension, so that the decisions which you make will have far-reaching consequences whether you are blocking relationships in your life or whether you are opening them up. The result of your choices reverberates throughout the Spirit dimension."

[20] After that conversation, Jesus carefully instructed his followers not to tell anyone that he was the Messiah.

The way is not easy

[21] Only after his understudies recognized that he was the Messiah did Jesus tell them what he was facing. He explained how he had to go to Jerusalem and to be falsely accused and judged by the rulers, the religious leaders, and the interpreters of the rules. He predicted his death and his resurrection on the third day. [22] When Peter realized what he was saying, he led Jesus to one side and began shouting at him, "This cannot be!" [23] Then Jesus turned and addressed Peter sternly, "Get away from me, you devil! Your denials offend me because they show how insensitive you are to God's way. You are responding from a human perspective."

[24] Against the background of his death and resurrection, Jesus began teaching his understudies what it meant to be associated with him. "If anyone will enter into my way of life, he must say no to his pseudo-self, take a constant attitude of death to all that is false, and follow after me. [25] If anyone tries to preserve a phony life, he will eventually forfeit it; if anyone will forfeit his phony life for me and the style of life I

represent, he will discover real life. [26] Since so many consider real life to be wealth and prosperity, consider this question. What if a man should own everything in the world, all its wealth, and forfeit his own selfhood? Once a person has lost his 'self,' how could he ever get it back? [27] When the Representative Man appears in the splendor and fullness of his Father, along with all of God's special messengers, on that day he will award each person in accord with what he has done with his life. [28] Some of you standing right here will live to participate in this new manifestation of God's presence in history."

A mystical experience

17 [1] Six days later Jesus took the three understudies closest to him—Peter, James, and John—up to a mountain retreat where they could be alone. [2] There they witnessed Jesus experiencing an unexplainable spiritual transformation. His face and his clothing shone brilliantly like the sun. [3] Moses and Elijah also appeared to be talking with Jesus. [4] Excitedly Peter exclaimed, "Lord, what a wonderful experience this is! If you want me to, I will erect three tents here—one for you, one for Moses, and one for Elijah." [5] Even as Peter was talking, a cloud covered them and from it a voice was heard, "This is my Son, whom I love and who pleases me. Listen to what he has to say."

[6] When Peter, James, and John heard this voice, they were terrified and fell prostrate on the ground. [7] But Jesus, having a deep concern for them, touched them gently and said, "Come on, get up. There is no reason for you to be afraid." [8] Still shaking, the understudies opened their eyes, but to their surprise, they saw no one else there except Jesus.

[9] As they made their way down the mountain, Jesus instructed them, "Do not tell anyone about this experience until I am resurrected." [10] Puzzled, the understudies asked, "Why, then, do the interpreters of the rules say that Elijah must

come back first?" ¹¹ Jesus explained, "He must come first to get everything ready. ¹² But I tell you truthfully that Elijah has already made his appearance, yet he was not acknowledged and was even mistreated shamefully. That's the way it will be with me." ¹³ Then Peter, James, and John understood that Jesus was talking about John the Baptizer.

Jesus talks about faith

¹⁴ As Jesus and his understudies approached the crowd, a man came up to Jesus and got on his knees in front of him. ¹⁵ "Sir," he said, "I brought my son to you who at times seems to be under the power of a separate personality that splits him in two, causing him to have severe seizures." ¹⁶ The distraught father continued, "I asked your followers to make my son whole, and they could not."

¹⁷ Jesus said to them all, "O you unbelieving crowd. How long must you observe my actions? How long must I endure your lack of faith? Bring the boy to me."

¹⁸ Then Jesus healed the lad and made him whole once again. ¹⁹ Later the understudies asked Jesus in private, "Why were we unable to help the boy?" ²⁰ "Because you have so little faith," Jesus replied bluntly. "If your faith were no bigger than a tiny mustard seed, you could say to a mountain 'Move!' —and it would! All things would then be possible for you."*

²² While they were in the province of Galilee, Jesus said, "The Representative Man will one day be handed over to the authorities. ²³ They will execute him, but on the third day he will experience resurrection." His talk about being executed made his understudies sorrowful.

²⁴ Later on when they got back to the headquarters in Capernaum, the tax collectors asked Peter, "Does your teacher pay taxes?" ²⁵ Peter responded, "Of course." When he went into the house, which served as their headquarters, Jesus stopped

---

* Verse 21 is not included in the best manuscripts.

him and asked, "What do you think, Simon? From whom do governments get their taxes? From their own citizens or from foreigners?" ²⁶ Peter answered, "They get it from aliens." Then said Jesus, "Citizens under their government are free of taxation, aren't they? ²⁷ Although we're free, there's no need to create a scene. Go over to the lake and cast a line into the water. Take up the first fish you catch, open his mouth, and in it you will find a piece of money. Take the money to those who collect taxes, and give it to them for me and for you."

A new route to recognition and fulfillment

18 ¹ About this time in his ministry, Jesus' understudies came to him, asking, "Who will receive the greatest recognition and power in this new expression of the Spirit dimension?" ² With that, Jesus looked about the crowd and found a small child. He beckoned the child and put him down in the midst of them. ³ "I am speaking straight with you—unless you are changed in your attitude and behavior and become like little children in your trust, you will not participate in the Spirit dimension. ⁴ The person who learns to function with the simplicity of a child will receive the greatest recognition and power in the Spirit dimension.

⁵ "And whoever gives unconditional acceptance to the person who lives this way will be giving unconditional acceptance to me. ⁶ And anyone who creates obstacles for a person taking his first steps in the Spirit dimension would actually be better off if he had a huge rock tied around his neck and were thrown into the lake.

⁷ "As long as you live in this world, you will face hardship and pain. Those who create these hardships for you will suffer the consequences of their destructive behavior. ⁸ Don't create hardship or pain for yourself. If your hand or foot blocks you, get rid of it. By comparison, it is better to enter life deformed than to be normal and wind up in meaninglessness and despair. ⁹ And if your eye, for example, blocks your growth, it

is better to live with only one eye in this life than having two eyes to go into darkness and everlasting despair.

¹⁰ "Be sure that you watch your attitudes toward my followers, and don't reject anyone who is taking his first steps in the Spiritual dimension. While someone else's journey may differ from yours, I assure you that my Father has a guide for every person on his journey. ¹¹ And for that very reason, the Representative Man entered into the human dimension to help those who have lost their way find it again.

¹² "What do you think about this? If a farmer has a hundred sheep and one of them gets lost, don't you think he would leave the ninety-nine and go look for the one which was lost? ¹³ And how do you think he will feel when he finds the one sheep that was lost? Why, he will be ecstatic and more joyous than for the ninety-nine who were safe and sound. ¹⁴ Just as the shepherd searches for one lost sheep, so will the Father search for one person who has lost his way, because it is not his will that a single person should finally be lost.

Getting clear relationships

¹⁵ "Let me talk with you about opening up blocked relationships. Suppose a brother of yours functions in a manner that creates negative feelings in you. Go to your brother and tell him how you feel. If he hears you and is sensitive to your pain, you have deepened your relationship with your brother. ¹⁶ If he does not hear what you say, invite a friend or two to sit together with you to mediate the relationship. Both of you will get a clearer picture when there are other viewpoints. ¹⁷ If under these circumstances there is no response from your brother, then share it with those who are in your fellowship of faith. If he will not respond to the spiritual community of faith, then you will have to leave him alone.

¹⁸ "I remind you again that decisions which you make have far-reaching consequences whether you are blocking relationships in your life or whether you are opening them up. The

[65

result of your efforts reverberates throughout the Spirit dimension. ¹⁹ I have told you this before: If two of you can be in harmony concerning something that you really want, ask my Father, the source of the Spirit dimension, and he will enable it to happen. ²⁰ And remember, where just two or three of you assemble in my Spirit, I am personally present with you."

Jesus explains forgiveness

²¹ After that Peter asked Jesus, "How many times am I to forgive my brother when he acts unloving toward me? Seven?" ²² Jesus responded, "Yes, forgive him seven times, then seventy times seven, or until you lose count.

²³ "Relationships in the Spirit dimension may be compared to a certain banker who was reviewing his debtors. ²⁴ While reviewing their accounts, he found a man who owed him millions of dollars. ²⁵ Because the man did not have any money to pay his note, the banker ordered the court to lock him up, along with his wife and children, and to take everything he had. ²⁶ When the debtor realized what was happening, he was shaken to the core of his being and pleaded with the banker, 'Sir, if you will give me time, I promise to pay everything I owe you.' ²⁷ The banker was so moved by the debtor's plea that he told the officer to release him, and he counted the loan paid off.

²⁸ "Upon leaving the bank, that very debtor walked out and found one of his fellow businessmen who owed him a few dollars. He grabbed him, shook him, and began choking him, saying, 'Pay me what you owe me.' ²⁹ And this fellow human being got down on his knees and begged him, saying, 'If you will just give me a little time, I will repay you every cent I owe you.' ³⁰ His pleas were to no avail, and his brother had him jailed until he could repay the loan.

³¹ "When some of his neighbors saw what he was doing, they told the banker all about it. ³² Then the banker called his debtor again and said, 'You ungrateful and insensitive man! I

wiped out the huge loan you owed me because you asked me to. ³³ Don't you think that you should have shown tenderness and caring for your fellow man, just as I showed compassion to you?' ³⁴ The banker was extremely angry and had the man put into solitary confinement until he could pay everything he owed. ³⁵ This story depicts something of how your heavenly Father will deal with you when you do not forgive your fellow human being his unloving acts."

God's purpose in marriage is permanent unity

19¹ When Jesus had finished talking to his followers about forgiveness, he left Galilee and went back into Judea, which is on the other side of the Jordan River. ² Great crowds continued to follow him, and he regularly healed those who were afflicted.

³ Back in Judea, a group of the Rulekeepers began interrogating him by asking, "Can a man get a divorce for any reason he desires?" ⁴ "Don't you know what the record says?" Jesus replied. "In the very beginning, the Creator made human beings male and female. ⁵ In the basic structure of creation, it is designed for a man to separate himself from his father and his mother and to be joined to his wife. Their union will create a new unit of society. ⁶ After they are married, they are no longer two separate individuals, but constitute a new unity. When God so joins two persons, nobody should separate them."

⁷ "Well," they said, "why did Moses say that if a man wishes a divorce, let him put it in writing, give it to his wife, and send her on her way?" ⁸ Jesus explained, "Because of your insensitivity to each other and the destructiveness of your relationships, Moses instructed you how to terminate a marriage, but that is not in accordance with God's original purpose. ⁹ I tell you, whoever sends his wife away without evidence that the relationship is already broken and dead, then marries another woman, commits adultery."

¹⁰ His understudies were stunned by this statement. "If what you're saying is so, it seems to us that it would be better for a man never to marry." ¹¹ Jesus acknowledged, "Not everyone can accept the challenge which I am about to offer. ¹² There are different reasons for a person's not having an active sex life. By birth, some persons may have no sexual desire. Others may be castrated by men, and still others may sublimate their sexual desire through their work for God. If you can accept this challenge, then do it."

¹³ On another occasion, some eager parents brought their little children to Jesus hoping that he would lay his hands on them and pray over them. Some of his understudies reacted negatively to the parents and told them to go away. ¹⁴ But Jesus said, "Don't put down the good intentions of these parents. Encourage them to bring their children to me because they symbolize the Spirit dimension." ¹⁵ And Jesus gently placed his hands on the children. When he had finished praying for them, he left.

The danger of wealth

¹⁶ One day a young man ran up to Jesus and asked, "Good teacher, what must I do to live forever?" ¹⁷ Jesus answered, "First of all, why do you describe me as 'good'? God is the only truly good one. But in response to your question, if you really want to live, function according to the rules." ¹⁸ "Which ones?" he wanted to know. Jesus said, "You shall not destroy another person, you shall not have sex with anyone but your wife when you marry, you shall not take what belongs to somebody else, you shall not lie about another, ¹⁹ respect your parents, and you must love every other person as you love yourself." ²⁰ Quite confidently the young man responded, "I've been doing all of these ever since I was a child. Why do I feel that something is still wrong with me?" ²¹ Then Jesus directed, "If you really want to be complete, sell all of your possessions

and distribute the money to those who don't have any. That will enable you to reorder your values. Then follow me, and you will experience authentic life." ²² When the young man heard Jesus' explanation, he was depressed and turned and walked slowly away, for he was extremely wealthy.

²³ As Jesus watched him walk away, he turned to his understudies and said, "I am communicating straight with you when I say that a wealthy person will have great difficulty entering into the Spirit dimension. ²⁴ It is much easier for a camel to get on his knees and crawl through the low gate in the wall of the city than for a wealthy person to give himself unreservedly to God's purpose." ²⁵ When his understudies heard this statement, they were so shocked that they asked Jesus, "Who then can be made whole?" ²⁶ When Jesus saw their consternation, he said, "True wholeness cannot be achieved by a person in his own strength, but anything and everything is possible with God."

The understudies' reward

²⁷ Peter reflected on what Jesus had said and raised this question: "Look, we have given up all our possessions to be with you and to understand your message. Now, what will we get out of it?" ²⁸ Jesus responded, "I am very straight with you when I promise you followers of mine that in the recreation of all things, when the Representative Man exercises both power and authority, you, too, will have power and authority guiding and directing the twelve tribes of Israel. ²⁹ Not only you, but everyone who leaves his home or brothers or sisters or parents or wife or children or possessions of any kind for me will get it all back a hundred times over during this life, and then he will truly have deathless life—the life of the ages. ³⁰ But remember this, many who are prominent and powerful in this life will go unnoticed in the next. And many who are powerless and poor today will rule in the life to come."

God's way is not man's way

20 ¹ "Life in the Spirit dimension may also be compared to a man who functioned as a manager. At six o'clock one morning, the manager arrived at the labor pool to hire workers for the vineyard. ² After he had negotiated an acceptable day's wage, he put them to work. ³ Again, about nine o'clock, he walked by the labor pool and saw several men standing idle. ⁴ He said to them, 'If you will put in the rest of the day working in my vineyard, I will pay you an appropriate wage.' So they went to work. ⁵ He also went down to the labor pool about noon and at three o'clock in the afternoon and did as he had previously done. ⁶ Then at five o'clock he went past the labor pool and found still others who were idle. He said to them, 'Why have you not been working today?' ⁷ 'Because no one has given us a job,' they replied. He said, 'Go and finish out the day working at my vineyard, and I will give you whatever is appropriate.'

⁸ At six, the manager said to the treasurer of the company, 'Call all of the workers together and pay them off, beginning with those I hired last.' ⁹ And those who were hired at five o'clock and had only worked one hour were paid the same wage as those who had worked all day. ¹⁰ When those who had worked all day came to receive their checks, they naturally felt that they deserved more than those who had worked only one hour, but they received the same thing. ¹¹ When they looked at their checks, they began complaining about the manager's injustice. ¹² They reasoned, 'These men who worked one hour have been paid the same as those of us who worked not only longer, but during the heat of the day.' ¹³ The manager responded, 'My good men, didn't you receive the agreed-upon wage? ¹⁴ Take what you have earned and go on home. I will pay these who worked but one hour the same that I paid you. ¹⁵ Can't I do with my resources whatever I please? If I choose to be generous with these who have as great a need as you,

why do you call my generosity evil?' " ¹⁶ Jesus explained, "Many who enter the Spirit dimension late will actually have priority, and those who originally had priority will lose it."

A call to service, not status

¹⁷ Jesus continued his journey toward Jerusalem, and on the way he invited his understudies to sit down a few minutes to rest. While they were resting he said, ¹⁸ "We are now on our way to Jerusalem, where the Representative Man will be handed over to the official religious leaders and the interpreters of our rules, who will hold court and sentence him to death. ¹⁹ They will then hand him over to the non-Jews who will humiliate and beat him and nail him on a cross. But the third day, he will experience resurrection."

²⁰ After this interlude, they continued on their journey, and the mother of two of his understudies, James and John, approached him with reverence and respect to ask him a favor. ²¹ Jesus inquired of her, "What do you want from me?" She said, "Permit my two sons to have places of recognition and authority when you establish your new government for our nation." ²² Jesus answered, "Your request is founded upon a lack of accurate information about who I am and what I am about to do." He turned to the other disciples and asked, "Can you stand the test of loyalty which I am about to stand? And can you endure the suffering and pain which lie before us?" They responded, "Yes, we can." ²³ "Yes, you will stand the test of loyalty which I am to endure and you will experience the pain and suffering which lie before me, but the right to delegate places of recognition and authority is not mine to give; that is a decision which my Father makes."

²⁴ When the other ten understudies recognized that James and John were seeking to be elevated over them, they were furious. ²⁵ After Jesus had settled them down, he said, "You are aware that among the non-Jews, there is a hierarchy of power. Those in our own country exercise power and authority

over us, but then they have others who exercise power and authority over them. ²⁶ That is not the way to hold true power, but whoever would have the greatest power and authority, let him serve others. ²⁷ And whoever would like to have the greatest power and recognition must become a humble servant. ²⁸ Pattern your life after the Representative Man, who did not come to exercise power and authority over others, but rather came to serve and to give his life for many."

Jesus restores sight

²⁹ By this time they had passed through Jericho on the way to Jerusalem, and a large crowd was accompanying him. ³⁰ Just outside Jericho, there were two blind men who sat beside the road every day, asking for contributions from those who passed by. When they heard that Jesus was in the midst of the crowd going by, they began to cry out in unison, "Help us! Help us! Oh, Lord, the offspring of our father, David, help us!" ³¹ The crowd began to shout at them, "Shut up, shut up." The louder the crowd roared, the louder they cried, "Help us! Help us! Oh, Lord, offspring of David." ³² Above the roar of the crowd, Jesus heard their request and called to him. "What do you want me to do for you?" he asked. ³³ They said to him, "Lord, we want to see. Heal our eyes." ³⁴ Jesus was deeply moved by their request. He reached out his hands, touched their eyes, and immediately they were healed. These two men then joined in the crowd which was following Jesus up to Jerusalem.

Jesus' unforgettable entry into Jerusalem

21 ¹ On their way to Jerusalem, they stopped at Bethphage and the Mount of Olives. There Jesus chose two of his understudies ² and said to them, "Go into the next town, and there you will find a donkey and her colt tied together. Untie them and bring them here for me. ³ If anyone questions you, just answer, 'Our leader needs these animals,' and that person will promptly let them go." [4] This incident fulfilled what one of the ancient writers had said: [5] "Let Jerusalem know that her ruler is coming, riding in humility on a donkey and on a colt, the donkey's offspring."

[6] The two understudies followed Jesus' instructions. [7] They brought the donkey and her colt to him, and after they had spread their clothes on the animals, Jesus mounted the colt for the trip. [8] Part of the crowd followed their example and began spreading their garments along the road, while others cut off palm branches and scattered them in his path. [9] Everyone in the crowd, both behind and in front of Jesus, began to cheer, "Celebrate the order initiated by our father David, which is reinstituted in this man! Celebrate this one who represents the Lord! Celebrate life to the fullest!"

[10] When Jesus entered Jerusalem with his entourage, he created quite a stir, so that the people kept saying to one another, "Who is this? Who is this?" [11] And the crowd began to chant, "This is Jesus, this is Jesus, the prophet of Nazareth from Galilee."

[12] Upon entering Jerusalem, Jesus went straight into the building which was dedicated to the worship of God. He put an end to the buying and selling of goods by overturning the tables at which the bankers were making change to the other salesmen. [13] Angrily he shouted, "Our spiritual leaders of old wrote, 'The building dedicated to the worship of God will be known as a place of prayer,' but you have turned it into a disreputable marketplace."

[14] By this time a number of deformed and crippled persons had learned that Jesus was in the temple. They came to him for help, and he made them whole. [15] When the religious officials and the interpreters of the rules observed what Jesus was doing, and when they heard the little children running through the building crying, "Recognize and honor David's son, recognize and honor David's son," they were threatened and angry. [16] These leaders approached Jesus and asked, "Do you hear

[73

what these kids are saying?" Jesus responded, "I surely do, but haven't you read in those records which you keep interpreting that God has said, 'Even the children and the babies who nurse their mothers will offer perfectly acceptable worship'?" [17] With that statement, Jesus left Jerusalem and went out to the small community of Bethany to spend the night.

More on faith

[18] Leaving Bethany the next morning without any breakfast, he became hungry on the way to the city. [19] In the distance he saw a fig tree growing along the roadside, but when he got to it, he found no fruit at all, only leaves. With a deep feeling of frustration he declared, "You will never produce fruit!" Immediately the fig tree began to wilt. [20] His understudies stood there in amazement and whispered to one another, "Look how quickly that fig tree is withering!" [21] Using the incident to teach a lesson, Jesus said, "I emphasize to you that if in your life you have faith which produces a clear vision of reality, you will not only speak to fig trees that are barren, but you will have authority to command mountains, saying, 'Depart and be cast into the sea,' and it will be done. [22] And everything you present to the Father with utter trust in him will come to pass."

Jesus rebukes the religious leaders

[23] Later on when he was in the building which was dedicated to God, the religious officials and the decision makers for the nation challenged his teaching. "What right have you to interfere with the order of life we have? Who gave you the right to function as you are?" they asked. [24] "Since you are interrogating me," Jesus replied, "I also will interrogate you. You answer my question, and I will answer yours. [25] Tell me, was the baptism that John administered done according to God's purpose, or was it John's own creation?" The leaders withdrew

for a brief discussion. They said, "If we say it was according to the will of God, his next question will be, 'Why didn't you submit to his baptism?' ²⁶ But if we say it was John's own idea, think what the people may do to us, because they believe that John was an authentic representative of God." ²⁷ After their talks, they reported to Jesus, "We choose not to disclose the answer to your question." Jesus responded, "Well, I choose not to answer yours, either."

²⁸ Then Jesus continued his dialogue with the religious leaders. "Tell me what you think of this story," he said. "Suppose there was a man who had two boys. He said to the older, 'Son, I want you to work with me in the business today.' ²⁹ The boy answered, 'I don't want to.' But after he thought about it for a while, he changed his mind and went to work with his father. ³⁰ After speaking to his older son, he came to the younger and made the same request of him. Without any hesitation, the younger son said, 'Yes, sir, I'll be glad to help you.' But he never showed up all day. ³¹ Which of these two boys did what their father really wanted?" The pious Rulekeepers responded, "The first." Jesus affirmed their answer and pointed to a far-reaching principle. "The tax collectors and women who sell their bodies for money will participate in the Spirit dimension before you do. ³² You see, when John appeared telling you how to relate to God and to each other, you didn't trust what he was saying. But the tax collectors and the women who sell their bodies trusted what he had to say. And even after you had seen the results of his work, you didn't change your mind and trust what he taught.

The Establishment's power will end

³³ "Let me tell you another story that emphasizes the same idea and expands on it. Once upon a time there was a large landowner who decided to plant a vineyard on his land. After he fenced in the vineyard, he built a winery, and beside the

winery he built a tower from which he could observe the fur-
thest corner of the vineyard. He then leased the vineyard to
managers and set out on a trip around the world.

[34] "In the course of his journey when he realized it was time
for his vineyard to bear fruit, he dispatched some of his employees to go to the managers and ask for a percentage of the
profit from the vineyard. [35] But the managers killed one of
these employees and beat the other two unmercifully. [36] Then
the landowner sent several more employees, but the managers
treated them just as badly as they had the first group. [37] Finally, the landowner had no one left to send but his only son.
Thinking to himself, 'Surely these managers will respect my
son,' he sent him to the vineyards. [38] When the managers saw
the son, however, they began to plot together, saying, 'Look.
This boy will inherit the vineyard and all this land. Let's kill
him; then we can take over the land for ourselves.' [39] So they
apprehended the son, dragged him out of the vineyard, and
murdered him. [40] Now, when the landowner returns, what do
you think he will do to those managers?"

[41] They replied, "He will fire them and prosecute them to
the limit; then he will find other managers to take care of his
property, someone who will give to him his share of the vineyard when it is ripe." [42] Jesus said, "You are professionals in
the religious business, and you understand the teachings which
our fathers have given us. Did you ever notice this statement
of the ancients—'The large stone which the mason continued
to cast aside, that very stone was eventually chosen as the
cornerstone of the building—that choice is so astounding it
must be God's own action.' [43] Here is the point of my story:
the direction of God's work in the world will be taken away
from you and will be given to others who will return its pro-
duction to him."*

[45] When the religious officials and the Rulekeepers had heard

---

* Verse 44 is not in the best manuscripts.

all these stories, it became quite obvious that he was describing them and their attitude toward him. [46] They wanted to arrest him and put him in jail, but they feared the anger of the crowd because the crowd was more and more convinced that he was an authentic spokesman of God.

Don't approach the Spirit dimension casually!

22[1] Jesus continued to teach those who gathered in the house of God, and he continued to tell them stories which had symbolic meanings. [2] "The Spirit dimension can be compared to a certain president who prepared for his son's wedding. [3] He decided on the date and commissioned his staff to write invitations and mail them to a selected guest list. However, despite the R.S.V.P., nobody responded. [4] The next time he was more specific and requested his staff to invite personally those on the guest list: 'Tell them that I have made an elaborate preparation for the celebration; I've prepared a feast and I want them to come to the wedding.' [5] This time some of the selected guests made jest of the invitation and went about their activities as usual. [6] Those who were not preoccupied ridiculed the members of the president's staff, abused them terribly, and finally killed them. [7] When the president heard what had happened, he called out the army and executed those persons and burnt down their property. [8] He then said to the members of his staff, 'The marriage celebration is ready, but those persons who were invited did not desire to come. [9] Therefore, go issue a general invitation to anyone who wishes to attend the marriage of my son.' [10] So the members of his staff went out and invited every citizen. Many responded—good people and bad people, poor and wealthy, famous and unknown—and the wedding party was overrun with guests.

[11] "After the party got underway, the president came into the large ballroom to see the guests, and he saw a man sitting down to eat who was not properly attired. [12] The president said to him, 'My friend, why did you come here without proper

attire for this occasion?' The man was so frightened he couldn't say a word. ¹³ The president then told one of the guards, 'Arrest this man. Put handcuffs on him and lead him out into the street and let him wander aimlessly about. Let him feel the full consequences of his irresponsible behavior."¹⁴ Many will be invited to share the Spirit dimension, but few will prepare themselves for such a celebration."

Jesus avoids entrapment

¹⁵ While Jesus was telling this story, the pious Rulekeepers held a caucus to discuss how they could force Jesus into a contradiction. ¹⁶ When he had finished the story about the president and the wedding, they sent representatives from their group along with some representatives from the supporters of Herod, saying, "Teacher, we know that you are an authentic person, and you are teaching faithfully the ways of God. You don't care what people think about you; neither do you set one person above another. ¹⁷ Being certain of the integrity of your response, give us your opinion. Is it proper for us to pay tax to the Roman government or not?"

¹⁸ Jesus was listening not only to their words, but to the intent of their questioning, and he responded, "Why are you trying to trap me, you phonies? ¹⁹ Give me a piece of the money with which you have been paying taxes." They handed him a silver dollar. ²⁰ He asked, "Whose image is stamped on this coin? And whose inscription is written around its edges?" ²¹ They answered him, "The Roman emperor and his inscription." Replied Jesus, "Give to the Roman emperor the things that belong to him, and give to God the things that belong to him." ²² The simplicity and directness of his answer struck them so forcefully that they gave up trying to trap him.

God is God of the living

²³ No sooner had they left than some of the religious aristocrats, who do not believe in resurrection, came to him. ²⁴ They

asked him, "Teacher, you are familiar with the rules which Moses handed down to us. He said, 'If a man marries and dies before he has any children, his brother ought to marry his wife and have children for the sake of his brother who died prematurely.' [25] We have a case in point where there were seven brothers. The first one married, died prematurely, and having no children, his brother married his widow. [26] This brother died, then the third and the fourth and on until all seven had married this woman. [27] Finally, the woman died. [28] Now at resurrection, whose wife will this woman be since each of these men married her and were properly joined to her?"

[29] Refusing to be caught in their trap, Jesus said, "Your problem is essentially your lack of understanding of what God has taught you and the power which he has. [30] In that form of existence beyond resurrection, persons will neither marry nor establish families, but rather be in the immediate family of God, even as those who are now in his presence. [31] With regard to the reality of resurrection, do you not know what God himself has said? [32] 'I am God of Abraham and God of Isaac and God of Jacob. God is not the God of nothing, but of something; not the God of nonbeing, but of true being.' " [33] When the crowd heard this response, a shocked hush fell over them.

Two rules for life

[34] When the pious Rulekeepers got word that Jesus had neutralized the attack of the aristocrats, they swore again to trap him. [35] This time they sent a lawyer as their delegate to ensnare Jesus. [36] The lawyer asked, "Teacher, among all the rules which we have been given, which do you consider superior?" [37] Without any hesitation Jesus answered, " 'You are to love the Lord your God with all your feelings, with all your inner being, and with all your intelligence.' [38] This is the number one rule. [39] And the second rule is quite similar. 'You will love every person just as you love yourself.' [40] These two basic rules

[79

form the foundation of all the lesser rules and other teachings declared by the speakers for God."

⁴¹ While Jesus had the ear of the Rulekeepers, he proposed a question to them. ⁴² "What are your opinions about the Messiah? Whose offspring is he?" They responded immediately, "He is the offspring of David, our king." ⁴³ "If that is true, how does David, by the inspiration of the Spirit of God, address the Messiah as Lord? ⁴⁴ Remember that he said in one of the Psalms, 'God the creator said to the Christ, "Take your place of authority next to me till everything that contradicts you has been subdued." ' ⁴⁵ Since David addressed the Messiah as his Lord, how can the Messiah be his child?"

⁴⁶ Not a one of the Rulekeepers was able to open his mouth, and from that day on, not a one of them interrogated him again.

Jesus denounces their perversion of the law

23 ¹ After the above encounter, Jesus continued to teach the crowd, along with his understudies. ² "Those interpreters of the rules and the Rulekeepers are successors to Moses. ³ Listen to their instructions and do what they tell you to do, but don't pattern your behavior after theirs because they are better proclaimers than they are practitioners. ⁴ For example, they pile up rules and regulations that weigh you down like a marble slab, but they don't keep those rules any more than they would try to lift a marble slab with their little finger. ⁵ These pious Rulekeepers are professional actors. They play their parts and say their lines to elicit positive responses from their audience. They identify themselves by their costumes since you could never recognize who they are from the way they live. ⁶ That's why they like to sit at the head of the table during the festivals and have the front seat in the worship service. ⁷ And that's why they carry out their ritual greetings on the street and encourage people to call them 'teacher' or 'instructor.' ⁸ I don't want anyone to call you 'teacher' because there is only one teacher for you, and that is the Christ. All of you are equal; you are brothers and sisters.

⁹ "And in that same line of thought, don't consider anyone your father on this earth in the sense that he is the source of your life, because you have only one Father who is the source of your being. ¹⁰ Don't place yourselves in roles of authority over each other because there is one in authority over all—the Christ. ¹¹ Remember what I tried to teach you before: 'The greatest fulfillment of your life will come from serving each other.' ¹² The person who sets himself up as superior to others will evoke jealousy and anger, and he will be brought down. On the other hand, the person who identifies with the people and accepts his common life with them will be recognized by life's source.

¹³ "Beware, you interpreters of the rules and you pious Rule-keepers, you actors! Beware of the fate that awaits you. You make it very difficult for persons to experience the Spirit dimension. For all of your words about real life, you don't live it.* ¹⁵ Beware of your faith, interpreters of the rules and Rule-keepers, you phonies! You send missionaries to the ends of the earth to convert unsuspecting persons to your way of thinking, and in so doing, you distort their life and destroy their being.

¹⁶ "Beware of your fate, you blind leaders! You say, 'It's not binding if a person swears by the house of God, but if he swears by the gold in God's house, it is binding!' ¹⁷ You are so ignorant and insensitive! Which is of more importance, the gold itself or the house of God which has the gold in it? ¹⁸ In the same way, you have a rule that says, 'It isn't binding if a person swears by the altar in God's house, but if anyone swears by the gift that is laid upon that altar, it is binding.' ¹⁹ You ignorant, insensitive leaders! Symbolically, which has greater power, the gift or the altar that consecrates that gift?

---

* Verse 14 is not found in the best manuscripts.

²⁰ Whoever swears by the altar certainly swears by everything that is connected with it. ²¹ Whoever swears by God's house not only swears by it, but by God who dwells in it. ²² And whoever swears by whatever is ultimate swears by God's authority and his very person.

²³ "Beware of your fate, you interpreters of the rules, you pious Rulekeepers, you phonies! Because of your interest in money, you are willing to give ten percent of the tiny spices like mint and anise and cummin, but you totally reject what is really important—justice, kindness, and trust. You should give priority to these character traits without neglecting the other. ²⁴ You are such blind leaders with inverted priorities. You choke at a gnat and swallow a camel.

²⁵ "Beware of your fate, you interpreters of the rules, you pious Rulekeepers, you phonies! In your approach to life, you clean up the exterior, but you leave the grease and grime of extortion and impurity on the inside. ²⁶ You are so blind. If you clean the grease and grime that is on the inside, the external appearance will take care of itself.

²⁷ "Beware of your fate, you interpreters of the law, Rulekeepers, you phonies! You remind me of neatly kept and whitewashed tombstones which appear immaculate on the outside, but on the inside are full of bones, death, dirt, and decay. ²⁸ You are careful to live according to the rules so that everything will look right to your fellow man, but surely you are aware that your performance is not connected to your feelings, thus the contradiction in what you do and who you are.

²⁹ "Beware of your fate, you interpreters of the rules, you Rulekeepers, you phonies! You are very careful to preserve the graves of the speakers for God and to identify the places where good people have been buried. ³⁰ You often lament, 'If we had been contemporaries with these good and godly people, we would not have persecuted and killed the speakers for God as our forefathers did.' ³¹ In that very acknowledgment

you are identifying yourselves as descendants of those who murdered the speakers for God. That's tantamount to a confession of what you will do. [32] In the most complete way possible, you will carry out your forefathers' tradition of getting rid of the speakers for God. [33] You are a group of self-deceivers, a generation of beguilers. How can you escape the consequences of the contradiction in your being? [34] Somewhere it is written in our records, 'I will send speakers to you, persons of wisdom, interpreters of my plan. Some of these you will kill, some you will even beat in the places of worship, and others you will expel from one city after another.' [35] And you will be held accountable for all your actions reaching all the way back to the beginning of time when a good man, Abel, was slain, right down to Zechariah, son of Barachiah, a man who was killed in God's house right beside the altar. [36] I'm straight with you when I say the consequences for all these rejections will be experienced by this generation of people.

Jesus' despair over Israel's indifference

[37] "Jerusalem, O Jerusalem, you who represent my nation, you have killed God's spokespersons, you have persecuted and rejected those he has sent to you. Time after time as I have looked at you, I would have healed your divisions and protected you just as a hen pulls together her chicks and protects them with her wings, but you would not permit me. [38] I have made my final appeal to you, and now I leave you to your fate! [39] I will not appeal to you again, and from this time on you will not see me; in fact, you will not see me until you say, 'We are now ready to accept the man who comes as God's spokesperson.' "

A time of extreme testing is coming

24 [1] After issuing these warnings directed both toward the pious Rulekeepers and his understudies, Jesus left God's house. As they left, his understudies said, "Look how big God's

house is and how finely it is decorated." ² Jesus said, "You see how large it is and how well it is constructed. I am speaking straight to you when I say, 'Not one stone of that building will be left in place, but the entire structure will be destroyed.' "

³ They walked out of the city, and Jesus sat down on the Mount of Olives to rest. While he was relaxing, his understudies came to him without the presence of a large crowd. They said, "Tell us when God's house will be destroyed. And also, tell us about your coming again (whatever that means); and describe to us what the climax of history will look like."

⁴ Jesus answered, "Here are some things you need to consider. Beware of illusions, both your own and those of other persons. ⁵ While you are looking for my appearance in the future, you could be confused by the illusions of those persons who claim to be the Christ. Many will buy their line. ⁶ Before this era comes to completion, there will be a number of active wars and the threat of many more. Do not be anxious for your own security during these times, but realize that wars will take place before the climax of history. ⁷ There will be strife within nations, and there will be strife and war between nations. Nations will lack food, there will be plagues of insects and pests, and there will be natural calamities like earthquakes and storms in different places. ⁸ These events will mark the beginning of your testing and pain.

⁹ "In addition to the general threats I have outlined, you will personally be arrested, tortured, and many of you will be killed. Sometimes you will feel hated by everyone because you have associated yourself with me. ¹⁰ During these periods of severe testing, many will turn from their commitment to me. Some will identify family members to an enemy, while others will actually hate their relatives. ¹¹ Many phonies will appear who claim to be God's spokespersons, and they will convince a following with their delusions. ¹² Because the power of destruction will be so intense, the motivation which love inspires

will wane in many persons. But the person who perseveres to the completion of the age will find personal wholeness and fulfillment. [14] And the good news of the Spirit dimension will be told throughout the earth so that every nation will have an opportunity to respond to it. Only then will the climax of history come about.

A time terrible beyond words

[15] "Now regarding the utter destruction of this house of God, whenever you see the most irreverent, unholy act imaginable (an act which Daniel, God's spokesman, has described) transpiring in this consecrated place, [16] if you are in Judea at that time, evacuate the city and hide in the mountains. [17] During that crisis, give priority to your physical safety. Should you be on top of the house either resting or repairing the roof, don't even come down. [18] If you should be in the field working, don't even pick up a shirt you have pulled off. [19] Those women who are pregnant or who are nursing babies will have a very difficult time evacuating the city with haste. [20] Do hope and pray that this event does not take place in winter, nor on the consecrated day when you are not supposed to travel. [21] During the time that I am describing, there will be great pain and suffering, the kind of misery which persons have never known before and truly will never know again. [22] This period of suffering and pain will be so intense that no human being could survive, yet for God's own people, he will shorten those days and preserve their lives.

[23] "Note especially in those days of suffering if a person says, 'The Christ is here or the Christ is there'; don't believe it. [24] During times of suffering and persecution, many will pretend to be the Christ and many will pretend to be the spokesperson for God; they will even be able to perform magic. There will be such a facsimile of the Christ, they almost will convince God's chosen people, but you know they can't do that. [25] Remember, I have told you about all these things. [26] If

these deceivers say, 'Look here, he's in the desert,' don't go out looking for him. Or if they say, 'Look, he's hiding in a closet,' don't believe that, either. [27] For like the flash of lightning in the sky will be the appearance of God's Representative Man. [28] Just like birds of prey are inwardly drawn to their food, so will you be to me.

History's climax in God's hands

[29] "Right after the pain and suffering of the days I have described, you will observe strange signs in the natural order. There will be an eclipse of the sun and of the moon and a number of shooting stars, and it will appear to you that the sky is falling around you. [30] At that time, there will appear again in the heavens God's Representative Man. When he does appear, all persons on earth will recognize him and be sorry for their behavior which has contradicted his way. And they shall recognize the Representative Man because of the authority and power which is invested in him. [31] When he arrives, he will commission his associates with the blast of the trumpet, and they will summon his people from the four corners of the earth and from the whole universe.

[32] "Now learn this symbolic lesson from the fig tree. When a fig tree begins to bud and send forth its leaves, you are aware that summer is not far away. [33] Likewise, when you see all of the things I have described taking place, you will know that my reappearance is very near, like someone knocking at your door. [34] When these things take place, the people who see and experience them will not die until everything I have said has come to completion. [35] The earth and sky may disintegrate, but the promises and predictions which I have made will stand.

[36] "But let me remind you, no person knows exactly when the climax of history will come—I mean not a single person, not even God's special messengers, but my Father only. [37] The

spirit of revelry and irresponsibility will characterize the era when God's Representative Man returns. [38] Just before the great flood people were banqueting and partying and getting married up to the very day that Noah entered the huge boat. [39] The persons of his day had no idea what was happening until the flood swept them away. It will be like that when God's Representative Man returns. [40] Also, as in Noah's time, there will be separation. Two persons may be working in the yard, and one of them will be taken, the other not. [41] Two women may be working in the factory; one of them will be taken and the other one left behind. [42] I instruct you, be alert everyday, for you do not know the exact time when the Christ will come again. [43] You know that the owner of a house would keep watch if he had any idea what hour of the night the burglar would break in, but he never knows when the burglar will come. [44] In similar fashion, you must be ready at every hour of the day or night, for at the very moment that you think Christ is not coming, he will appear.

The faithful will be rewarded

[45] "You may be wondering just who will be recognized as a trusted and favored servant of Christ, one who will receive his reward at the appropriate time. [46] Consider the analogy of employer and employee. How fulfilling it is to an employer to have an employee do what he is supposed to do without constant supervision. [47] You know that an employer will elevate such an employee to a management position because he can be trusted. [48] On the other hand, suppose an employee begins to imagine, 'My employer is nowhere in sight, so I don't have to concern myself with him.' [49] Suppose also that this irresponsible employee creates confusion and a strife with his fellow employees, stays out of work, and develops a number of self-destructive habits. [50] The employer will show up just when the employee is least expecting him, when he has no

idea of his appearance, [51] and he will fire that employee, giving him a very low evaluation to anyone who asks. It will be obvious to anyone in the labor market that he is unworthy of a job. Consider what unhappiness and loss and suffering this will bring him.

Stay alert

25 [1] Early the next morning, the top religious and civil leadciple of the Spirit dimension. Reality may be compared to ten bridesmaids. [2] Five of these made proper preparation for the wedding, while five neglected to do so. [3] Those who were foolish took their lamps full of fuel, but they took no extra fuel. [4] Those who prepared themselves properly not only filled their lamps with fuel, but took extra fuel also. [5] Because the bridegroom did not come along immediately, all of them went to sleep. [6] As the night wore on, there was a sudden loud cry, 'Prepare yourselves, the bridegroom is coming. Go present yourselves to him.' [7] All the young ladies rose, picked up their lamps, and began lighting them. [8] Those who had not prepared themselves said to the others, 'Share your fuel with us, for our lamps have gone out and we cannot relight them.' [9] To this, the others responded, 'No, we cannot share our fuel with you because then we too will run out. Go and buy extra fuel and come back.' [10] Those without fuel went to purchase some. While they were gone, the bridegroom came. Those who were prepared presented themselves to him, and he took them into his house. [11] Later on, the five young women who had not prepared themselves came knocking at the door, 'Sir, sir, open the door to us also.' [12] The bridegroom responded, 'Really, I don't know who you are,' and he would not open the door. [13] The point of this story is that you must be alert at all times and in all experiences of your life because you do not know the moment when the Representative Man like a bridegroom will be coming to meet you.

Use your talents productively

¹⁴ "Here's a story which illustrates another principle of the Spirit dimension. This principle may be compared to a man who was going overseas on a trip, and he called in his employees and gave each of them a portion of his assets. ¹⁵ He gave to one employee $5,000, another $2,000, and still another $1,000. He gave to each person an amount of money equal to his/her ability. The next day he departed on his trip.

¹⁶ "The person who had received $5,000 invested it carefully and doubled its worth. ¹⁷ The person who had received $2,000 did likewise and gained $2,000 more. ¹⁸ But the person who had received only $1,000 put it into a safe-deposit box, neither using it himself or making it available to others.

¹⁹ After the employer returned home from his trip, he set a day in which he would have an accounting of their investments. ²⁰ The employee who had received $5,000 reported that he had invested the money carefully. In his report he said, 'Sir, you gave me $5,000, and I have been able to double its value. I present to you the original $5,000, plus $5,000 more.' ²¹ His employer said, 'You have done a good job. You are a prudent and faithful employee. Because you have managed a small investment well, I will entrust to you greater and greater responsibility. Share my sense of fulfillment with me.'

²² "The employee who had received $2,000 came to his employer and said, 'Sir, you gave me $2,000, and I was able to gain $2,000 more by wise investment.' ²³ The employer said to him, 'You have done a good job and you are truly a capable employee. Since you have been diligent with a small sum, I will entrust to you the management of greater resources. Share with me the fulfillment which I have in your behavior.'

²⁴ "Finally, he came to the person who had only $1,000. This person said, 'Sir, you are a hard investor to compete with. I know you can get a return when you don't even make an investment, and you can harvest a crop without cultivating it

properly. ²⁵ Knowing how astute you are, I was anxious about my own ability. So I took the $1,000, and put it in a safe-deposit box. Here's your original $1,000.' ²⁶ The employer said, 'You are a frightened, irresponsible employee. You know that I am a sharp businessman, making wise investments and harvesting large crops, and I have given you a very clear model. ²⁷ You should therefore have invested the money which I gave you so that, upon my return, I would have the original investment plus the increase.' ²⁸ He then turned to an officer and said, 'Take the $1,000 this man has and give it to the man who had $10,000. ²⁹ Every person who manages his assets wisely will be given additional assets so that he may have an abundance. But the person who does not manage his assets wisely will lose those he has. ³⁰ Dismiss this stupid employee and let him wander in confusion and meaningless suffering as the consequence of his careless behavior.' "

The final accounting

³¹ Then Jesus said to his understudies, "At the climax of history you can expect the return of the Representative Man, and at that time, he will exercise total authority and he will be accompanied by the special messengers of God. ³² At that time, he will assemble all the nations of the earth and he will separate time from each other just as a shepherd separates sheep from goats. ³³ And he will place the sheep to his right, and the goats to his left. ³⁴ Then with God's own authority he will beckon those on his right hand, 'Come along with me, those of you who have been fulfilled by my Father; take your place in this ultimate form of being, a place marked out for you since the first moment of creation. ³⁵ You see, I was hungry and you fed me; I was thirsty, and you gave me something to drink. I was unknown to you in many of our encounters, and you accepted me. ³⁶ I was without clothes, and you gave me clothes; I was sick and forsaken, and you visited me. I was locked up in jail, and you took time to be with me.'

[37] "At that time, those to whom he is speaking will ask, 'Sir, when did we see you hungry and give you something to eat; or thirsty, and give you something to drink; [38] and when did we meet you as one unknown to us and invite you into our houses; or when did we see you without clothes and give you clothes? [39] When did we see you sick or in jail and visit you?' [40] And then the Representative Man, with the authority of God, will respond, 'I tell you the truth, and when you did any of those things to any human being, especially those without position or power, you were doing it to me personally.

[41] "With that, he will say to those on the left, 'Take your leave. Go away from me. Your being is under a curse, and you must experience the fate of all who reject the ultimate plan and purpose of God. [42] You see, I was hungry and you didn't give me anything to eat. I was thirsty and you didn't offer me a drink. [43] I was unknown to you and you didn't risk inviting me in; I was without clothes and you didn't give me any; sick and in jail, and you never came to where I was.' [44] These will protest, saying, 'Sir, when did we see you hungry or thirsty or a stranger or without clothes or ill or in jail and did not respond to your need?' [45] He will answer, 'I tell you the truth, when you had the opportunity to do these things to any human being, especially to those without position and power and you did not do it, it was the same as not doing it to me. [46] Those who did not relate to the needs of their fellow human beings with sensitivity and concern will suffer inestimable loss. Those who did respond will experience authentic life age after age."

The plot against Jesus

26 [1] When Jesus had concluded these special instructions to his understudies, he said to them, [2] "You are aware that in a couple of days we will be celebrating the feast which commemorates our nation's deliverance from Egypt, and at that time, the Representative Man will be handed over to his enemies to be killed."

³ About that time, the top religious leaders, which included interpreters of the rules and the decisionmakers of the people, met in the executive office of the chief religious leader, whose name was Caiaphas. ⁴ They struck on a plan whereby Jesus would be abducted without notice and killed. ⁵ By unanimous consent they concluded, "We must not apprehend him on the feast day because we might create a riot beyond our ability to control."

A loving gesture

⁶ After instructing his understudies, Jesus went out to Bethany, both to eat and to rest in the house of a man named Simon, who had been a leper. ⁷ While he was there, a woman came to him carrying a large bottle filled with an expensive perfume, and she poured it over his head while he was eating dinner. ⁸ When some of his understudies saw what she had done, they were quite angry. They asked, "Why this extravagance? ⁹ This perfume could have been sold for a good price and the money given to feed the poor."

¹⁰ When Jesus perceived their reaction, he chided them, "Why are you criticizing this woman? She has made a generous contribution inspired by love. ¹¹ Society will always have poor people, and rightly you should care for them, but since you don't have me with you always, her charitable gift may well take precedence. ¹² She has poured this perfume on my head and my body as a preparation for my death and burial. ¹³ Remember this—wherever you tell the good news of my coming, recount to the world what this woman has done, as a tribute to her for her trust and generosity."

Betrayal

¹⁴ It was about this time that one of Jesus' followers, Judas Iscariot, went to the religious leaders. ¹⁵ He said to them,

"How much will you pay me to hand Jesus over to you?" They put out a contract on Jesus for about thirty silver dollars. [16] From the time of that contract, Judas looked for a chance to hand him over to his enemies.

The final meal

[17] On the first day of the festival, the day that they ate bread without any yeast, Jesus' understudies came to him with a question: "Where do you want us to prepare the festival meal?" [18] He replied, "Go into town and find this certain man. Tell him, 'Our leader says that his time has come, and he wishes to celebrate the festival meal at your house.' " [19] The understudies followed Jesus' directions and prepared the meal to celebrate the Exodus.

[20] Later that evening, as Jesus sat around the table talking and eating with his understudies, he said to them, "I know that one of you will hand me over to the religious authorities." [22] This statement greatly upset the group, and each man began asking, "Am I the one, Lord?" [23] Jesus answered, "One who has shared my food in this room will turn me in. [24] The Representative Man will die as the ancient writers predicted, but the one who betrays him will suffer so much that he'll wish he had never been born." [25] Judas, the traitor, asked Jesus directly, "Am I the one?" And Jesus answered him, "You have said so."

[26] During the meal Jesus took a large piece of bread, prayed over it, then broke it into pieces and passed it around to the understudies, saying, "Eat this bread; it is my body." [27] Then he took a cup of wine and, acknowledging God as the source of all things, passed it around the table, saying, "I want each one of you to drink from this cup [28] because it is my blood that symbolizes the new relationship between God and his people, and it is my blood that will enable sins to be forgiven. [29] I say to you truthfully that I will not celebrate again with

you until history is fulfilled and we can celebrate together the ultimate fulfillment of creation."

³⁰ After the group sang a hymn, they went to the Mount of Olives. ³¹ Jesus told them what to expect: "Tonight every one of you will be ashamed of your relationship with me, just as the record says: 'When the parents are removed, the children go to pieces.' ³² But after I am resurrected, I will meet you in Galilee." ³³ Peter staunchly declared, "Everyone else may let you down, but I won't." ³⁴ Jesus replied sadly, "Peter, before the rooster crows at dawn, you will have denied your relationship to me three times." ³⁵ Still Peter asserted, "Why, I would die for you! I'll never turn my back on you!" So said all the other understudies as well.

Jesus prays for fulfillment of God's purpose

³⁶ By this time they had arrived at Gethsemane, and Jesus said to the understudies, "Wait here while I pray." ³⁷ He asked Peter, James, and John to be with him during his period of sorrow and deep stress. ³⁸ He confided to them, "My anguish is almost more than I can bear. Stay near me and be with me in my struggle."

³⁹ He went a few more steps, then fell to the ground and prayed, "Father, if there is any other way, spare me from this horror I am facing. Yet more than I desire to be spared, I want your purpose to be fulfilled." ⁴⁰ When he returned to the three understudies, he found them asleep. Disappointed, Jesus said to Peter, "I thought surely that for me you could stay awake one hour. ⁴¹ Be strong and try not to give in to this weakness again. Be aware of the conflict between what you feel at the moment and what you choose as the higher good."

⁴² Then Jesus went apart again and prayed, "Father, if there is no other way except for me to endure this trial, then may your purpose be fulfilled." ⁴³ And a second time he found the three understudies asleep, because they were very tired. ⁴⁴ A third time Jesus went off by himself and prayed the same

prayer as before. ⁴⁵ When he returned to where his followers lay, he said to them, "How long are you going to sleep? The time has come for me to die; the Representative Man will be turned over to his enemies. ⁴⁶ Get up, it's time to go. The one who is performing this act of treachery is coming now."

Jesus is arrested

⁴⁷ Even as he was talking, Judas approached him, accompanied by a large crowd carrying swords and clubs. The crowd had been put up to it by the top religious leaders and the national leaders. ⁴⁸ Judas had set up a signal for the betrayal: "The one I kiss is the one you should take away." ⁴⁹ Coming right up to Jesus, Judas said, "Greetings, teacher!" Then he kissed him quickly.

⁵⁰ Jesus looked directly at him and said quietly, "I know that you must do what you have come to do." Then the authorities grabbed Jesus and took him into custody. ⁵¹ One of Jesus' followers grabbed his sword and with a slashing motion cut off the ear of an employee of the chief religious leader. ⁵² Immediately Jesus spoke up and said, "Put away your sword! If you live by violence, you will die by violence. ⁵³ Don't you realize that I could ask my Father for special protection and he would give it to me? ⁵⁴ But how then would the record be fulfilled?" ⁵⁵ Then he addressed the crowd: "With all those weapons, it appears you have come to capture a hardened criminal. For days I taught in God's house, and you didn't seem to think I was dangerous then. ⁵⁶ But everything that is happening now is in fulfillment of the ancient record." At that moment the followers completely abandoned Jesus and ran off into the darkness.

Jesus and Caiaphas

⁵⁷ His captors took Jesus to Caiaphas, the chief religious leader, who was waiting with the interpreters of the rules and the civil officials. ⁵⁸ Peter had followed along at the edge of

the crowd until they got to the home of Caiaphas. Then he stood in the yard with some of the soldiers to see what would happen. ⁵⁹ All of the religious leaders who gathered inside were trying to find persons to testify against Jesus, that is, lie under oath so convincingly that he could be given the death sentence. ⁶⁰ Though they found persons willing to testify, their stories contradicted each other. Finally, two of the witnesses agreed. ⁶¹ They said, "We heard this man Jesus say that he could destroy God's house, then rebuild it in three days." ⁶² On hearing this, Caiaphas turned to Jesus and asked, "What do you have to say about that? Can you defend your statement?" ⁶³ But Jesus didn't say a word. Caiaphas prodded him, saying, "In God's name, I order you to tell me if you are the Messiah, the Son of God." ⁶⁴ This time Jesus answered, "You have said so. But I tell you this, that in the future you will see the Representative Man expressing the authority of God and radiating the energy of the Spirit dimension."

⁶⁵ Then Caiaphas tore his clothes in anger and shouted, "Blasphemy! We don't need to hear from anyone else. You have heard his sacrilegious words. ⁶⁶ What shall we do to him?" Others at the court answered, "Kill him! Kill him!" ⁶⁷ Then they started spitting on Jesus, beating him and slapping him. ⁶⁸ Tauntingly they asked, "If you have the powers of God's Son, tell us who hit you!"

Peter's moment of truth

⁶⁹ All this time Peter was sitting out in the yard. One of the housemaids approached him and asked, "You were one of those with Jesus, weren't you?" ⁷⁰ Frightened, Peter lied and said, "I don't know what you're talking about." ⁷¹ He moved to another part of the yard, but a maid there said the same thing—"This man was with Jesus." ⁷² Again, Peter swore vehemently that he did not know him. ⁷³ A little while later, several of the men standing in the yard accused him directly, saying, "We can tell by your accent that you are from Galilee.

You are one of them!" ⁷⁴ Then Peter began to curse and swear. "I told you I don't know him!" he said. At that moment a rooster crowed, ⁷⁵ and Peter recalled what Jesus had told him: "Before the rooster crows at dawn, you will have denied your relationship with me three times." Overwhelmed with remorse, he left the courtyard and cried with sorrow from the depths of his being.

27 ¹ Early the next morning, the top religious and civil leaders of the nation held a consultation to discuss how they could get rid of Jesus. ² They decided to bind him and take him to Pontius Pilate, the Roman governor of the province, and place him in his custody.

Judas' sad fate

³ By this time Judas, who had turned Jesus over to the Jewish authorities, was feeling guilty and condemning himself. He changed his mind about his behavior and took the thirty silver dollars back to the leaders. ⁴ "I am wrong because I have handed over to you a man who is innocent," he pleaded. But they rejected him coldly, saying, "Your guilt feelings are of no concern to us. That's your problem!" With his heart full of regret, ⁵ Judas threw down the thirty silver dollars on the temple floor, walked out, and committed suicide.

⁶ When the religious leaders had gathered up the money, they said, "It's not proper for us to place this money back in our treasury because it has been payoff money resulting in the death of a person." ⁷ After consulting awhile, they decided to buy a plot of ground on the edge of the city in which to bury strangers. ⁸ And from that day until this, that plot of ground has been called the Field of Blood, because of the money which was paid toward an innocent man's death. ⁹ There was a prediction of all this from one of God's spokesmen, Jeremiah, when he said, "And they took the thirty silver dollars, the price that was paid for his betrayal, the value that

the nation Israel placed upon him, ¹⁰ and they bought a burial plot for strangers as the Lord had intended."

"Kill him, Kill him!"

¹¹ By this time Jesus had been brought before the governor, who asked, "Do you consider yourself to be the new ruler of the Jewish people?" Jesus replied, "You have said so." ¹² At once, the religious leaders began to present their case against Jesus, but he didn't offer a single word. ¹³ Then Pilate said, "Don't you hear how many things they are testifying against you?" ¹⁴ Jesus still did not answer the governor, and his calm was a marvel to Pilate.

¹⁵ It was customary at the Feast of Passover for the governor to release one prisoner chosen by the people. ¹⁶ At that time there was in custody a notorious criminal named Barabbas. ¹⁷ While Pilate was talking to Jesus and the religious leaders, a huge crowd had gathered to witness this incident. Pilate then asked, "Whom do you desire that I set free today? Barabbas or Jesus, who calls himself the Christ?" ¹⁸ Pilate had already recognized the anxiety of the Jewish leaders, and that they wanted Jesus put out of the way for their own safety because they were envious of his influence and popularity.

¹⁹ Pilate went over and sat down on the bench at which he made official pronouncements. While he was sitting there, he received a communication from his wife which read, "Don't make any decisions about that innocent man. Because of him, my dreams have been disturbed of late." ²⁰ While Pilate was reading the note, the religious leaders convinced the crowd that they should request the release of Barabbas and demand the crucifixion of Jesus. ²¹ After he read his wife's note, the governor turned to the crowd and asked, "Which of these two men do you want me to release today?" Instantly they said, "Barabbas." ²² Then Pilate asked, "What do you wish me to do with Jesus, who calls himself the Christ?" With a roar they shouted, "Kill him!" ²³ "Why," Pilate asked, "what has he

done wrong?" Ignoring his question, they began to chant, "Kill him, kill him, kill him!"

²⁴ When Pilate recognized that he could not change their minds, he took a pan of water and washed his hands in the presence of the chanting crowd. Symbolically he was saying, "I am washing my hands of all responsibility in the death of this innocent person, and I want you to know that." ²⁵ The people declared, "Let the responsibility for his death be on us and on our children." ²⁶ He handed Barabbas over to them and when he had ordered Jesus to be beaten, he then ordered his crucifixion.

²⁷ With that order, the soldiers led Jesus into the assembly hall and gathered the whole battalion around him. ²⁸ They stripped his own clothes from him and clothed him in a scarlet robe. ²⁹ Then they plaited a crown made of thorns and pressed it upon his head. In his right hand they placed a reed like a scepter, and they began bowing to him like a king and mocking him, saying, "Hail to the chief, the king of the Jews!" ³⁰ They continued to taunt Jesus and spit in his face. Taking the reed out of his hand, they beat him over the head with it.

³¹ When the soldiers had finished their mockery, they took away the scarlet robe, put his own clothes back on him, and began a long procession out to the place where he was to be killed. ³² On the way, they pulled a man out of the crowd, Simon of Cyrene, and they made him carry Jesus' cross. ³³ Finally they got to the place where he was to be killed—Golgotha, "the place of a skull."

The Representative Man dies—for our sake

³⁴ Before they nailed Jesus to the cross, they tried to give him a mixture of vinegar and drugs to kill the pain; but when he tasted it, he would not drink it. ³⁵ After they nailed his body to the cross, they took his clothes and rolled dice to see who would get them. ³⁶ Then they sat down to keep a close watch on him. ³⁷ On a small board nailed to the cross was written

this inscription: "This is Jesus, the King of the Jews." [38] There were also two criminals who were crucified along with Jesus, one on the right side and the other on the left.

[39] The crowd began to dance and form lines to mock and revile him while he was suffering there. [40] They scoffed, "You said you could destroy the temple and rebuild it in three days. Well, deliver yourself. If you really are the Son of God, loose yourself from that cross." [41] Not only was he jeered at and derided by the crowd, but the religious and civil leaders also said, [42] "He delivered others, but he cannot deliver himself. If he is the king of our nation, let him deliver himself from that cross; then we will believe his message. [43] Remember how he trusted in God. Let God deliver him. But God won't have anything to do with him even though he said, 'I am the Son of God.'" [44] The two criminals who were being crucified with him joined in the mockery, along with the crowd and the leaders.

[45] About noon the sun was eclipsed, and it was dark until about three in the afternoon. [46] About three o'clock, Jesus cried out loudly, "My God, my God, why have you left me alone?" [47] The words that he had spoken were misunderstood by some who were nearby because they thought he was calling for Elijah, one of God's spokespersons. [48] In response to his suffering and agony, one of the crowd filled a sponge with vinegar for a sedative and placed it on the end of a cane pole, and offered it to Jesus. [49] The remainder of the insensitive crowd stood by, saying, "Well, let's see if Elijah will come and deliver him." [50] Once again Jesus cried out in anguish, then gave up the struggle, and died.

[51] With the death of Jesus there was a symbolic ripping of the veil in the temple, the veil that separated the masses of the people from the immediate presence of God. His death was also accompanied by an earthquake and a disruption of the forces of nature. [52] The earthquake opened the graves of many holy persons who had died long ago. [53] After Jesus' resurrec-

tion these even came out of the graves and went into Jerusalem and showed themselves to many people. [54] When the Roman soldier and the others who were standing around looking at Jesus felt the earthquake and all these things happening, they were really frightened and said, "In reality, this must have been the Son of God."

[55] A number of the women who had been following Jesus were observing these events at quite a distance. [56] Among these women were Mary Magdalene; Mary, the mother of James and Joseph; and also the mother of Zebedee's children.

A tender burial

[57] About sundown Joseph, a rich man from Arimathea, who was also one of Jesus' followers, went to Pilate. [58] He requested the privilege of burying Jesus, and Pilate released the body to him. [59] Joseph took the body off the cross, wrapped it with a clean piece of linen cloth, [60] and laid Jesus' body in a new tomb in a cave which he had recently prepared as a tomb for himself. Then he rolled a large stone over the entrance of the cave and went home. [61] He left Mary Magdalene and the other Mary sitting on the ground at the door of the cave.

[62] The day after they had killed Jesus, the religious leaders, along with the pious Rulekeepers, asked for a conference with Pilate. [63] They stated, "We remember what this impostor said when he was alive. He declared, 'After three days, I will experience resurrection.' [64] Please issue an order that guards be placed at the cave in which he is buried until after the third day. This will prevent his followers from stealing the body during the night and then declaring to the people, 'He has risen from the dead.' This latter error would certainly be worse than the former." [65] Pilate agreed and said, "Since you have sentries who can guard the cave, you have my permission to guard it as carefully as you can." [66] So these Jewish leaders went out to the tomb, sealed the entrance, and placed guards there to observe what happened.

[101

Jesus fulfills his earthly life

28 ¹ When the Jewish day of rest had ended and the dawn of the first day of the week began to break, Mary Magdalene and the other Mary went out to the cave where Jesus was buried. ² There was a shaking and tremor of the earth. God's special messenger came and rolled the stone away from the cave and was sitting there on top of it. ³ His face was luminous and his clothes were white like snow. ⁴ The guards whom the Jewish leaders had placed there were so paralyzed with fear that they appeared to be dead. ⁵ The messenger from God spoke to the women: "Do not be afraid. I know that you are looking for Jesus who was killed. ⁶ He is no longer in this cave. He has been resurrected just as he said. Come, look at the slab where they laid him. ⁷ Then go with haste and tell all his followers that he is resurrected. Explain to them that he is on the way to Galilee, and they will see him there just as I am telling you." ⁸ The women left the cave quickly, their feelings a mixture of fear and overwhelming joy. They literally ran to tell his followers the message which had been given them.

⁹ While they were making this trip, quite unexpectedly Jesus himself confronted them. When he said, "Hello, there!" the startled women turned aside and came directly to him, grasping him by the feet and worshiping him. ¹⁰ Jesus said to them, "Do not be afraid. Tell my understudies that they are to go together to Galilee, and they will see me there."

¹¹ While the women were reporting to the understudies, the guards who had been at the cave went to the city and told the religious leaders everything that had happened. ¹² When the leaders consulted with the guards, they gave them a large payment of hush money and ¹³ instructed them to say, "His followers came during the night while we were asleep and stole his body." ¹⁴ The leaders also told the guards, "If for any reason this report comes back to the governor, we will intervene

on your behalf and make sure that nothing happens to you."
[15] The guards took the hush money and told the story as they
were instructed. And this is how the Jews continued to explain
the disappearance of Jesus' body.

Jesus commissions his understudies

[16] In response to the women's report, Jesus' eleven remaining understudies departed for Galilee and went to a mountain previously indicated by him. [17] When they saw Jesus, they were awed and worshiped him, though some still doubted.
[18] Jesus came close and spoke to them: "Complete authority has been given to me throughout the universe. [19] I commission you now to go into every nation on earth and teach everyone what I have taught you. Initiate them into your community of faith by baptizing them in the name of the Father, the Son, and the Holy Spirit. [20] Teach them also to obey my instruction, and be confident that I will be with you in every event of your life until the climax of history."

Mark

INTRODUCTION

Mark is generally conceded to be the first gospel written, and one which was used extensively later by Matthew and Luke as a major resource in their writing. Most authorities agree that its author was John Mark, a companion of both Peter and Paul on their missionary journeys, and he probably wrote it in Rome sometime in the decade following the death of Peter in A.D. 64. There is some dispute as to whether Mark ever participated in any of the Christ events personally (some think the reference to a young man in 14:51 was to Mark) or whether he depended solely on Peter and the oral traditions for his information.

Why did Mark write this first gospel? It is possible the church in Rome was going through a time of persecution by the Emperor Nero, and early Christians needed to have the story of Christ and the body of his teachings in some more substantial form than oral tradition. Or, Mark may have been written to settle the conflict between the Jewish and Gentile forms of Christianity, a conflict that was prominent in the Roman church. The more traditional Jewish Christians observed many of the Judaic customs and centered their understanding of Jesus on his role as the Messiah. The Gentile Christians, on the other hand, celebrated their freedom from the old customs and looked to Jesus as the Son of God through whose incarnation God's grace came to the world. Mark is in sympathy with the Gentile Christians, and his style of writing is in sharp contrast to Matthew, who was more in tune with the Jewish Christians.

Mark differs from the other gospels in several ways. It is characterized by brevity, both in the number of chapters and in the actual sentence construction. Mark's emphasis is on action; he focuses on Jesus' deeds rather than his discourses. He avoids the theological and mystical symbolism of John, and he writes more vividly and at a faster pace than either Matthew or Luke. While Mark talks *about* Jesus, he does not quote him directly at length. In fact, Mark quotes Jesus fewer times than any other gospel. Mark's Jesus is seen less as the Messiah foretold by ancient scriptures and more as the Son of God whose ministry on earth heralded the breaking in of the "Spirit dimension."

The structure which Mark gave to his gospel is generally the same as that found in the other synoptic gospels, with the exception of an opening birth sequence, which is omitted. Thus, Mark presents the major events in Jesus' life, his preaching and teaching, then his death and resurrection—almost all in narrative form (as contrasted with the numerous areas of discourse in Matthew).

The ending of Mark has long been a source of controversy. The oldest and best manuscripts end chapter 16 with verse 8, as I have chosen to do. Some versions of the scripture add verses 9–20, which deal with the post-resurrection appearances of Jesus, but these verses were not, in all likelihood, a part of the original text of Mark.

THE GOSPEL OF MARK

John prepares the way

1 ¹ Here's how the good news about God's Son, Jesus Christ, was first communicated. ² It was first announced by John the Baptizer, who followed the line of God's spokesmen of old. In fact, one of them wrote, "I will send my messenger before you to prepare the people to receive what you have to say. ³ He will be like a voice shouting throughout the desert, 'Get yourselves ready for the Lord's visitation.' "

⁴ John told residents of Judea and Jerusalem to change their attitude and direction. He baptized those who responded to his message and assured them that God forgave them. ⁵ A large number of the residents responded to his instruction, acknowledged their sins, and received his baptism in the Jordan River. ⁶ John was something of an ascetic, wearing rough clothes and eating the wild food of the desert. ⁷ He kept telling the crowds, "The person who succeeds me is more powerful than I am. I feel so humbled by him that I would be self-conscious untying his shoe. ⁸ Whereas I baptize your body with water, he will baptize your inner being with the Holy Spirit."

Jesus identifies with sinners

⁹ After John had made these pronouncements, Jesus came from his home in Nazareth of Galilee and was baptized by John in the Jordan River. ¹⁰ As he stepped out of the water, it seemed to him that the sky opened and the Spirit of God like a dove descended upon him. ¹¹ He heard God speak to him, saying, "You are my dear son; I am pleased with you." ¹² On the heels of this experience, the Spirit compelled him to withdraw into the desert in solitude.

¹³ Jesus was alone in that deserted country for more than a month. During that time he was tempted by the Adversary and encountered wild animals, but God's special agents strengthened him for his encounter and encouraged him afterward.

Jesus calls followers

¹⁴ After John was jailed, Jesus went into Galilee to tell the good news about the ultimate triumph of God's purpose. ¹⁵ He said, "This is a moment of fulfillment; the manifestation of God's purpose is breaking through. Change your attitude about yourself and about God. Believe the good news." ¹⁶ As he was walking by the Sea of Galilee, he saw two brothers fishing, Simon and Andrew. ¹⁷ Jesus challenged them to make a new decision about their lives. "Join me in fulfilling God's purpose, and you will affect the lives of others." ¹⁸ Without hesitation they joined Jesus in his work.

¹⁹ A little further down the lake he encountered Zebedee's sons, James and John. They, too, were fishermen and they were repairing their nets when he called them. ²⁰ Without hesitation they left their father, the servants, and the family business to join themselves to Jesus.

Jesus shocks his audience

²¹ This small group went into Capernaum. On the Jewish day of worship they went into the synagogue and Jesus began teaching. ²² The congregation was shocked by his boldness. He taught with his own authority without quoting the rabbis like the interpreters of the rules. ²³ In this particular gathering there was a schizophrenic man who interrupted Jesus in the midst of his lesson: ²⁴ "Let us alone, Jesus of Nazareth. Have you come to destroy our way of life? I recognize you as a special representative of God."

²⁵ Jesus said to the separated part of this man, "Be at peace

with yourself; let yourself be reunited." [26] The man responded with groans, with tears, and with a loud shout; then he seemed to be reunited within himself. [27] The whole congregation was amazed and excited. This incident provoked a flurry of questions: "What's going on here? What new teaching is this? With authority he speaks to persons divided within themselves and they become whole persons." [28] After this incident Jesus' reputation spread throughout the countryside.

[29] After this episode in the synagogue the group went into Simon's house. [30] Simon's mother-in-law had a fever, and this information was shared with Jesus. [31] He came into her room, took her by the hand, and helped her out of bed. Suddenly her fever was gone, and she prepared food for them.

[32] After sundown the entire community brought to Jesus their sick and distraught. [33] It appeared that everyone in town gathered outside the house. [34] Jesus healed many who were sick with different illnesses and made whole many distraught persons, while refusing to let them expose his true identity.

[35] The next morning he arose a good while before daylight, went out into a solitary place, and prayed. [36] When Simon and the others got up, they looked for him. [37] When they found him, they reported, "Everyone is looking for you." [38] Apparently oblivious to their statement, Jesus said, "Let us go on into the other towns and announce the good news about God's purpose to them because that is why I am here." [39] And he preached in all the places of worship throughout Galilee and made many persons whole.

[40] On one occasion a leper came to Jesus, kneeled in front of him, and pleaded, "If you will, you can make me whole." [41] As Jesus looked at him, he was deeply moved. He stretched out his hand, touched him, and said, "I will. You are made whole." [42] Instantly the man was cured of his disease. [43] At the moment of healing, Jesus gave him these instructions and sent him on his way—[44] "Don't publicize your healing, but go directly to the priest and make the appropriate offering which Moses pre-

scribed as evidence to them." ⁴⁵ Contrary to Jesus' directive, the healed man told everyone he met, starting such a blaze of publicity that Jesus could no longer go into the towns but withdrew into deserted areas of the countryside. Even there crowds from throughout the region came to him.

Jesus forgives sin

2 ¹ After several days, when Jesus returned to Capernaum, word spread throughout the town that he was back. ² Right away such a large crowd gathered at his house that there was no place even to stand. The crowd overflowed into the yard, and Jesus took this occasion to proclaim his message to them.

³ While Jesus was speaking, a man stricken with paralysis was brought to the house by four friends. ⁴ When they could not get the sick man through the crowd, they stripped the tiles from the roof and lowered him on his stretcher into the room where Jesus was standing. ⁵ When Jesus recognized the faith of these four friends, he said to the paralyzed man, "Son, your sins are forgiven."

⁶ In the crowd were interpreters of the rules, who copy and study the Hebrew scriptures. They reacted negatively to Jesus' remark and thought to themselves, ⁷ "Why does this man blaspheme? Only God can forgive sins." ⁸ Jesus sensed what they were feeling and thinking. "Why do you entertain this attitude in your hearts? ⁹ Which is easier to say to this sick man, 'Your sins are forgiven'; or, 'Get up, take your stretcher and go'? ¹⁰ So that you may be assured that the Representative Man has authority on earth to forgive sins, I will make this man whole." ¹¹ He said to the paralyzed man, "Get up, pick up your stretcher, and go home." ¹² At Jesus' instruction, he got up, picked up his stretcher, and walked off in full view of everyone. The crowd was awed and extolled God's act in the healing. "Never before have we experienced anything like

this!" they exclaimed. ¹³ And Jesus made his way to the sea-
side again, with the crowds following him. Again, he taught
them.

Jesus accepts social outcasts

¹⁴ On one of his trips, Jesus passed the tax booth of Levi,
the son of Alphaeus. Jesus said to him, "Follow me." And
Levi followed him. ¹⁵ He then invited Jesus to have dinner in
his home; he also invited a number of his colleagues and people with bad reputations. These social outcasts ate and drank
with Jesus and his followers, and a number of them decided
to associate with him. ¹⁶ But when the culturally elite interpreters of the rules and pious Rulekeepers observed Jesus'
practice of eating and drinking with these outcasts, they spoke
to his followers. "How can your leader eat and drink with
these social outcasts and violators of God's rules?" ¹⁷ When
his followers reported this query to Jesus, he responded,
"Those persons who are whole do not need a doctor, but those
who are sick. I have not come to change those who consider
they are right, but to enable those who are aware of their need
to change their lives."

New wine—new wineskins

¹⁸ Jesus had another encounter with the pious Rulekeepers.
Several representatives from that group said to Jesus, "We
fast. Even the followers of your friend John fast, but your followers are always eating and drinking. Why is this?" ¹⁹ Jesus
responded, "Can the friends of a groom fast on the eve of his
wedding? While the groom is around, they don't even consider
fasting. ²⁰ There will come a time when the groom is taken
from them and then they may choose to fast."

²¹ On another occasion Jesus illustrated the effect of his mission on individual lives and social structures. "No person
sews a piece of new cloth on an old piece of clothing because

when the new piece shrinks, the rip will be worse. ²² No person puts new wine in old wineskins because when the new wine ferments, the skins will burst and both the wine and skins will be wasted. New wine requires new wineskins."

People take precedence over rules

²³ On another occasion Jesus walked through the grain fields on the Jewish day of rest. His followers pulled heads of grain and ate them. ²⁴ Again, the Rulekeepers queried him, "Why do your followers break the rules?" ²⁵ And he referred them to what one of their respected leaders had done. "Don't you recall what David and his associates did when they got hungry on the sacred day? ²⁶ Remember how David went into the temple and ate the consecrated bread which only the priests are permitted to eat. What's more, he gave some of the consecrated bread to his companions. ²⁷ The day of rest was set apart for man's good, not the other way around. All the rules should be viewed in this way. ²⁸ Anyway, the Representative Man is the Lord of this sacred day (just as he is Lord of all the rules)."

Jesus gets recognition

3 ¹ On another sacred day Jesus went into the Jewish house of worship. A man with a deformed hand was present. ² Jesus' critics observed carefully to see if he would cure the man because they wanted this evidence against him. ³ He asked the man with the deformed hand to stand up before the congregation. ⁴ Jesus then addressed his critics: "Is it proper to do good on sacred days, or to do evil? Let me ask the question another way—Is it right to preserve life or to destroy it?"

His critics remained silent, and ⁵ he stared at them with anger and disgust because of their insensitivity to another human being. Then he spoke to the man: "Stretch out your hand." As he stretched it out, it became normal just like his other one. ⁶ Then the pious Rulekeepers took the data they gathered against Jesus and consorted with a political group who were loyal supporters of King Herod. Both these groups began to plot how they could get rid of Jesus.

⁷ While they were scheming, Jesus withdrew to the lakeside. Numerous persons from Galilee and Judea followed him. ⁸ A huge crowd gathered from Jerusalem, Idumea, the region beyond Jordan, and from Tyre and Sidon because they had heard of the astounding healings which had taken place. Some came out of curiosity while others came seeking wholeness in their own lives. ⁹ Jesus requested his understudies to prepare a small boat for him so he could avoid being pressured by the crowd. ¹⁰ Because he had made numerous persons whole, many in the crowd, hoping to be healed, pressed against Jesus just to touch him. ¹¹ Quite often persons who were in deep emotional distress tumbled on the ground before him, screaming, "You are the Son of God." ¹² But Jesus was quick to tell them to keep his identity secret.

Jesus chooses twelve understudies

¹³ One day Jesus went up into a mountain and invited twelve men to accompany him. ¹⁴ He then appointed these twelve to travel with him so they could observe his actions and listen to his message. After their training he intended to send them out to spread his message, ¹⁵ to heal the sick, and to make the broken whole. ¹⁶ The twelve included Simon, whom Jesus called Peter; ¹⁷ James, Zebedee's son, and John, his brother, whom Jesus nicknamed "the sons of thunder." ¹⁸ The others were Andrew; Philip; Bartholomew; Matthew; Thomas; James, Alphaeus' son; Thaddaeus; Simon the Cananaean, who formerly belonged to a violent revolutionary group; ¹⁹ and lastly Judas Iscariot, who betrayed Jesus.

[113

Jesus identified with the Adversary

²⁰ After Jesus selected these twelve and stated what he wanted from them, they went back down the mountain into his house. The crowd gathered again, making it virtually impossible for them to eat. ²¹ When Jesus' friends and family heard about his activities, they described him as being beside himself, and they sought to take him back home.

²² A group of interpreters of the rules from Jerusalem came down to Galilee where Jesus was teaching. They said, "He is possessed by Beelzebul, the chief ruler in the spirit underworld, and by that evil spirit he releases others from their possession." ²³ Jesus invited them to dialogue by asking, "How can the Adversary cast himself out? ²⁴ If a nation is split, it cannot continue. ²⁵ Or, if a household is split, it cannot continue. ²⁶ Therefore, if the chief of the underworld opposes himself, he is split and will lose his power. ²⁷ Consider this analogy. A burglar cannot enter the house of a powerful man and take his valuables and destroy the order of his household unless he first conquers the man who lives there. Then he can rob him of his valuables.

²⁸ "You need to be aware that persons will be forgiven all kinds of sins, no matter how heinous. ²⁹ If, however, persons deliberately and consistently identify the activity of the Spirit of God with the spirit of the underworld, they cannot receive forgiveness ever because they distort reality and lose their consciousness of God." ³⁰ Jesus made these statements because the interpreters of the rules identified his work with the Adversary.

³¹ On another occasion his brothers and his mother came to the place he was teaching and called out to him. ³² When Jesus did not respond, someone in the crowd yelled, "Your mother, your brothers and sisters are calling you." ³³ "Whom do you consider to be my closest relatives?" Jesus asked. ³⁴ Then as

114]

he looked from face to face, he answered his own question. "You are my closest relatives. ³⁵ Whoever fulfills the intention of God, that person is like a brother or sister or mother to me."

The farmer and his seed

4 ¹ On another occasion when he was by the lake, he started teaching his followers again. Because they were so numerous, he got into a small boat and sat there on the lake while the crowd stood along the shoreline. ² He presented his message in stories to help them grasp his meanings. ³ In one of his presentations he said, "Listen to this. A farmer began planting. ⁴ In the course of his planting, some of the seed fell on the hard path, and birds swooped down and ate these. ⁵ Some of the seed fell on a thin layer of soil with a thick rock ledge underneath. These sprouted quickly and came up immediately because they were planted near the surface. ⁶ But when the sun came up, these plants withered because they had no depth. ⁷ Some seed fell in the midst of thorns. These thorns grew with the good seed, choking the vitality out of the plants so that they never bore fruit. ⁸ Yet other seed fell on good soil. These sprouted, produced strong plants, and reproduced —some thirty, some sixty, and some a hundred times as much as the initial planting." ⁹ Jesus concluded, "If you can understand this story, appropriate its meaning for your life."

¹⁰ After the major portion of the crowd dispersed, he was left with the twelve and a few others who were attracted by his story which carried a spiritual meaning, and they asked him for an interpretation. ¹¹ He explained, "You who share this mission with me are to understand the mystery of the Spirit dimension, but those who are not participating with us receive only the stories. ¹² Those outsiders see the picture, but they don't grasp its meaning; they hear the words, but they don't understand their significance. If they did experience the meaning of the stories, their lives would be transformed and

their misguided actions forgiven." [13] Then he said, "If you do not understand this story, how can you understand my other stories?

[14] "Here's the explanation. The planter plants an authentic witness of God in every relationship. [15] Planting on the hard earth is like an encounter with a person whose response to the witness is superficial; thus, there is no penetration of his defenses. Immediately the Adversary snatches away the impact of the encounter. [16] Those persons who are represented by the thin layer of earth are those who immediately celebrate an encounter with an authentic communicator of God. [17] But the joy is short-lived because they do not open their inner being to the presentation of the Spirit, and soon the surface encounter withers. [18-19] Those seed sown among thorns are like encounters with persons who are possessed with wealth or pleasure, whose awareness is on externals, and these other interests quickly erase the impact of the encounter. [20] The seed sown on good ground are those encounters in which there is a real meeting of persons, those in which each feels himself or herself to be met by God. These seed then are received, they grow and bear fruit—some thirty, some sixty, and some a hundred times as much as the initial planting."

Your life can light others

[21] Jesus said, "Do you purchase candles to place under a tub or under your bed and not on a candlestick? (Obviously the light one obtains is to shine forth in every relationship.) [22] Let the light illuminate every relationship because eventually everything in life will become visible to everyone, and every secret will be broadcast for all to hear. [23] If you can understand this analogy, appropriate its meaning for your life." [24] Again, Jesus admonished his understudies—"Pay attention to what you hear! As you give forth, you will receive in return. [25] It is a law of spiritual growth that if you continue to open yourself to new possibilities, they will continue to come to

you. But if you close yourself to additional growth, what you have received will be lost."

Jesus describes the Spirit dimension

²⁶ Jesus continued, "The Spirit dimension is like a seed planted in the earth. ²⁷ A person plants it, then sleeps and rises night and day. The seed sprouts and grows, though the planter doesn't understand how. ²⁸ The earth has power to reproduce naturally—first the blade, then the stalk, and finally the full wheat. ²⁹ When the wheat matures, the planter gathers it in, because the harvest is ready.

³⁰ "Again, how shall I describe to you this Spirit dimension? To what can I compare it? ³¹ It is like a single mustard seed, which is one of the smallest seeds sown on earth. ³² After it is sown, it grows into the largest of shrubs. Its branches shoot out in such size that birds come to rest in its shadow."

³³ Using symbolic stories like these, Jesus endeavored to teach his followers about the Spirit dimension, careful to give them no more than they could handle. ³⁴ He always spoke to the crowds in stories, refusing to give them a concrete statement. But when he was alone with his understudies, he explained to them the special meaning of his stories.

A further revelation of power

³⁵ Late one evening, after teaching the better part of the day, he said to his followers, "Let us go over to the other side of the lake." ³⁶ They dismissed the crowd and pushed off from the shore with Jesus in the boat. (There were several small boats near them.) ³⁷ Suddenly a storm arose, and the waves tossed the boat about, filling it with water. ³⁸ During the storm Jesus was asleep in the stern. The understudies woke him, shouting, "Teacher, don't you care that we are in danger of drowning?" ³⁹ Jesus rose and spoke sternly to the wind and the sea, saying, "Settle down, be at peace." Immediately the wind stopped blowing and the sea quit churning. There was

a deep stillness. ⁴⁰ Then he spoke to his followers: "Why are you so frightened? Where is your trust?" ⁴¹ Afraid and perplexed, they questioned each other—"Who is this person that even the wind and the sea respond to his directive?"

Jesus reunites a fragmented personality

5 ¹ They crossed the lake and landed in the region of the Gerasenes. ² When Jesus got out of the boat, he was immediately accosted by a demented man who was living in the cavelike tombs common in that area. ³ He came dashing up to Jesus—he was so fierce that no person had been able to control him, not even with chains. ⁴ His countrymen had repeatedly tied him with chains and shackles, but each time he got loose. Nothing could restrain him. ⁵ Night and day he was in the mountains or inside the caves, screaming and cutting himself with stones.

⁶ When this tortured man saw Jesus at a distance, he ran to him and worshiped him. ⁷ Then he cried out at Jesus, "How am I related to you, Jesus, Son of the Most High God? In the name of God, please don't torture me any more." ⁸ Jesus responded, "Come out of this man, alien destructive spirit." ⁹ Then he said to that separated part of the man, "What is your name?" That part of him answered, " 'Many'—because my personality is split into many parts." ¹⁰ That separated portion of the man begged, "Do not banish me from this country." ¹¹ Near the mountain a herd of pigs was feeding. ¹² "Let us enter the pigs," said the separated parts, "if we must go." ¹³ When Jesus directed these fragmented parts to leave, they entered the pigs, making them dash headlong down a steep slope into the lake where they drowned. (There were about two thousand of them.)

¹⁴ The men who tended the pigs fled into the city and told what they had seen. People from the city and surrounding countryside went out to witness the incident for themselves. ¹⁵ They first came to Jesus; then they saw the demented man

quietly sitting beside Jesus, fully clothed and mentally together. They were frightened. [16] The witnesses related what
they had seen happening to the man separated from himself
and what had happened to the pigs. [17] The crowd began urg-
ing Jesus to leave their community. [18] Jesus responded by getting into the boat. The man who had been united with himself
pleaded with Jesus to permit him to accompany him. [19] Jesus
refused. "Go back home to your friends and tell them what
God has done for you and how he has cared for you." [20] The
healed man left and traveled throughout the region of the ten
cities, telling his remarkable story of what Jesus had done for
him. His hearers were awestruck.

Remarkable faith

[21] Jesus got into the boat and returned to the other side of
the lake. A crowd was gathered right up to the water's edge.
[22] Out of the crowd stepped a man named Jairus, an official
from the local synagogue. When he got to Jesus, he fell at his
feet [23] and pleaded, "My daughter is ill at home, and I fear
she is dying. Please come with me and lay your hands on her
body and heal her, so she will live." [24] Jesus responded to his
request and went with him, the crowd following closely behind.

[25] In the crowd was a woman who had had a menstrual problem for twelve years. [26] Though she had already been treated
by many doctors in the region, and had spent her last cent,
she grew no better but rather worsened. [27] The woman had
heard of Jesus' healing ministry, so she made her way through
the crowd and touched Jesus' clothes. [28] She had convinced
herself that "if I can touch his clothes, I will become whole."
[29] Indeed, when she touched him, her bleeding stopped immediately and she knew in herself that she was healed. [30] Jesus
sensed that healing power had gone out of him. He turned to
the crowd and asked, "Who touched me?" [31] His understudies
replied, "You see this crowd milling around you—it could have
been a dozen persons. How can you ask such a question?"

[119

³² Jesus studied the faces in the crowd to see who had made contact with him. ³³ The woman knew what had happened to her, and she was frightened as Jesus looked at person after person in the crowd. She anxiously stepped forward and fell down before him, confessing what had happened. ³⁴ Gently Jesus said to her, "Your trust has made you whole, daughter. Go your way in peace, and continue to be well."

³⁵ While he was talking with her, messengers from the official's house arrived and said to Jairus, "Your daughter is dead; don't bother the teacher any longer." ³⁶ When Jesus heard the report, he said to Jairus, "Do not panic. Only trust." ³⁷ For the remainder of the trip he permitted only Peter, James, and John to accompany him. ³⁸ When they came to Jairus' house they found confusion, with everyone crying and grieving. ³⁹ Upon entering he asked, "What is going on here? Why the uproar? This child is not dead; she is merely asleep."

⁴⁰ Their mourning suddenly turned to scorn when they felt themselves under attack. When Jesus had dismissed the mourners, he took the father and mother with his campanions into the room where the child was lying. ⁴¹ He then took her by the hand and said, "Little girl, get up." ⁴² Immediately she sat up and walked around—she was twelve years old. All those who witnessed it were overcome with awe. ⁴³ Jesus insisted that no one was to know about the incident. "Give the girl something to eat," he added.

The hometown people are resentful

6 ¹ After these incidents Jesus, followed by his understudies, went back home to Galilee. ² On the Jewish rest day he went to the religious gathering and taught there the same message he had declared in the countryside. The people were filled with wonder. "Where did he learn this wisdom? What is this peculiar power he has that enables him to heal people and change their lives?" ³ Then they said, "Isn't this the carpenter, Mary's son? Is he not the brother of James,

Joses, Judas, and Simon? Don't his sisters live here?" These hometown people resented Jesus. ⁴ He said to them, "A special spokesman for God meets rejection only in his home town among his relatives, friends, and family." ⁵ He was unable to continue his ministry of liberation except for healing a few sick persons. ⁶ It astounded Jesus that these persons he knew and loved did not trust him. Nevertheless, he continued going from one community to another teaching them about the Spirit dimension.

Commissioned for mission

⁷ After a while he brought together his twelve understudies. Dividing them into pairs, he commissioned them to share his ministry to persons and gave them authority over those forces which destroy persons. ⁸ He gave them instructions for their travels: "Do not take life's necessities with you; take only a walking stick—no bag, no bread, no money. ⁹ Wear shoes and take only one coat." ¹⁰ He continued, "When you enter a community, settle in a home that will accept you and stay with them until you leave. ¹¹ Do not be discouraged by those persons who are unresponsive to your message. When you leave, shed your feeling of responsibility and wipe the dust of remembrance off your shoes. You have given them my word; their response is their responsibility. On the final day of reckoning those persons will have no excuse."

¹² These twelve went out telling people that they should change their attitude about God and themselves. ¹³ Some of the signs that characterized Jesus' ministry appeared in his understudies: destructive spiritual forces were expelled from persons, and those who were sick got well.

The tragic death of John the Baptizer

¹⁴ Eventually the ruler, Herod, heard about Jesus because he was gaining a widespread reputation. Herod said, "This

[121

man is John the Baptizer whom I executed. He has come back to life, and that is why he is able to perform these awesome acts." ¹⁵ Rumors also had it that Jesus was Elijah or at least one of the spokesmen for God. ¹⁶ Herod, however, was obsessed with the idea that Jesus was John the Baptizer risen from death. ¹⁷ His obsession grew from the fact that he had imprisoned John at the insistence of his wife, Herodias, who was formerly married to his brother Philip. ¹⁸ For John had been saying to Herod, "It is not proper for you to have your brother's wife." ¹⁹ So Herodias nursed a grudge against John. John's judgment infuriated her, and she would have killed him instantly but she couldn't. ²⁰ Herod held John in high esteem, knowing that he was a dedicated man endeavoring to live the right kind of life. He was displeased when he heard John, but he was so convinced of his authenticity that he listened eagerly.

²¹ For his own birthday Herod gave a party and invited all the social, political, and military leaders in Galilee. ²² His niece (Herodias' daughter) danced for the company and delighted everyone present, and Herod said to her, "Request anything you desire and I will give it to you." ²³ He confirmed his pledge with an oath. "*Anything* you ask, I swear I will give it to you, even to half of my kingdom." ²⁴ She was stunned by the offer and consulted with her mother: "What shall I ask?" Her mother responded: "The head of John the Baptizer."

²⁵ She dashed into the party, ran up to the king, and said, "I want you to give me the head of John the Baptizer on a platter." ²⁶ Her request depressed the king, yet because he had given his word in the presence of his guests, he could not refuse her. ²⁷ Without reconsidering, he sent an executioner to the prison to behead John. ²⁸ Before the party ended, he brought John's head on a platter and gave it to the girl; she, in turn, gave it to her mother. ²⁹ When a group of John's followers heard about the incident, they came for his body and buried it.

Jesus feeds the crowd spiritual and physical food

[30] About this time the twelve understudies whom Jesus had chosen to share his work returned from their trip. They reported to him what they had been doing and teaching. [31] Because they were exhausted, he invited them into a deserted place to relax. This withdrawal was necessitated by the coming and going of the numerous persons being affected through the ministry—so many the understudies had little time even to eat. [32] They embarked in a boat to a place where they could find solitude. [33] When the people saw Jesus leaving, they anticipated where he would go and met him there. The crowd was quite large. [34] When Jesus got out of the boat, he saw what a sizable crowd had gathered, and his awareness of their needs moved him deeply. He perceived them as children without parents, and he began to parent them.

[35] Because of his intense concentration on the people, both he and they were oblivious to time. Finally, his understudies interrupted him: "It's getting late and there is no food here. [36] Dismiss this crowd so they can find food for themselves in the village or from friendly folk in the countryside." [37] Jesus said, "You give them something to eat." The understudies responded, "Do you want us to spend all the money we have for food and give it to them?" [38] He asked, "How many loaves of bread did you bring for us?" They checked and reported: "Five loaves and two fish." [39] Jesus told the crowd to sit down on the grass, and [40] they clustered in groups of fifty and one hundred. [41] Picking up the five loaves and two fish, he looked up into the sky and blessed the food, then broke the loaves and gave them to his understudies to offer to the crowd. Likewise, he divided the fish among them all. [42] Everyone present ate until he was satisfied. [43] After the meal they filled twelve baskets with leftover bread and fish. [44] About five thousand men ate the loaves and the fish that day.

Jesus again shows mastery over natural laws

⁴⁵ At once Jesus instructed his understudies to get back into the boat and return to Bethsaida while he dismissed the other people. ⁴⁶ Sending them home, he went up into the mountain to commune with God.

⁴⁷ Late in the evening the boat with his understudies was in the middle of the lake, and Jesus was alone on the mountain. ⁴⁸ From his position he could see them struggling with the oars because the wind was against them. Early in the morning he approached their boat by walking on the lake; he would have passed them by, ⁴⁹ but they saw him walking on the lake and mistook him for a spirit. ⁵⁰ Shuddering, they shrieked and were deeply stressed. He spoke to them at once, saying calmly, "Take heart, it is I; don't be anxious." ⁵¹ As he walked over to the boat, the wind ceased. These understudies were filled with immeasureable wonder and amazement. Awe pervaded their minds. ⁵² They had been unable to appropriate the meaning of the loaves and fish because their spiritual perception was dull.

⁵³ Jesus and his understudies went across the lake and landed in Gennesaret. ⁵⁴ As soon as they stepped out of the boat, the people recognized Jesus. ⁵⁵ They went throughout the area and began bringing their sick people to him. ⁵⁶ Wherever Jesus went, the people brought their sick to him. When they could not converse with him, they lined the road hoping to make even the least contact with him. Those who made contact became well.

Empty rituals

7 ¹ Then several interpreters of the rules, along with a group of pious Rulekeepers, came from Jerusalem to interview Jesus. ² They observed with a critical spirit that Jesus' understudies did not practice the customary ritual of handwashing before eating. ³ ⸤These pious Rulekeepers do not put food into their mouths unless they go through their hand-washing ritual; neither do Jews of any sect, for that matter, because they have a special loyalty to "the way we have always done it." ⁴ For example, if one of them has been to the supermarket, he will not eat unless he first goes through the washing ritual. In addition to this handwashing ceremony, they have a variety of washings they go through: washing pots and pans and tables, and so on.)

⁵ These pious Rulekeepers and these interpreters of the rules quizzed Jesus: "Why do your understudies disregard the traditions our fathers passed on to us? Why don't they observe the handwashing ritual before they eat?" ⁶ Jesus responded, "Isaiah perfectly described you actors when he said, 'This group affirms me verbally, but their words are disconnected from their feelings and actions. ⁷ Empty is this group's attempt at communion with me because their faith is nothing more than man's fabrication.' ⁸ You have disregarded the clear directives of God in favor of these manmade ways of living—like washing hands and pots and pans."

⁹ Jesus spoke explicitly, "Very clearly you are rejecting God's directive in order to keep doing what you have always done in the way you have always done it. ¹⁰ Let me point to one of your practices to illustrate what I mean. Moses as God's spokesman said, 'Respect and care for your father and mother because whoever dishonors his parents will suffer the consequences.' ¹¹ You nullify God's directive by your man-made ritual. For example, if your parents have needs, you make a pronouncement over your resources—'This is dedicated to God'—and by your ritual deny your parents what you possess. ¹² With this ritual you free yourself from responsibility for your parents. ¹³ With your manmade excuse, you nullify God's directive. This is but one example of the numerous ways you set aside God's directives to preserve your cultural patterns."

¹⁴ At this point in the discussion Jesus invited the crowd to

come in closer. "Listen to me—every one of you, listen—understand what I have to say. ¹⁵ Nothing outside a person entering into his awareness or experience can distort or pervert him; but that which originates in the inner being of a person and comes out through his/her actions—this can pervert. ¹⁶ If you grasp what I am saying, appropriate this truth for your life."

¹⁷ When Jesus entered the house to relax a bit, his understudies asked him to explain this symbolic statement. ¹⁸ "Do *you* not grasp the significance of these ideas?" he asked. "Don't you see that what enters into a person cannot distort because it is neither good nor bad in itself. ¹⁹ Things on the outside do not enter the feelings and motivation, but rather go into the stomach and pass into the intestines and out again." (This statement indicated that food and drink have no moral significance, so what a person eats or drinks does not define who he is essentially.)

²⁰ Jesus continued, "The behavior that originates in a person's inner being can distort him. ²¹ From the inside, out of the depths of a person, comes destructive behavior: negative thinking, sex outside of marriage, sex of any kind without commitment, destroying the lives of others, ²² taking another's goods or wanting to, blindness to others' needs, game playing, giving undisciplined expression to every desire, paranoid behavior, irreverence toward holy things, setting oneself above others, thoughtless or meaningless action—²³ all this destructive behavior arises in the depths of a person and is motivated from his very being. Functioning in these ways distorts and destroys a person."

²⁴ After offering this instruction to his understudies, Jesus went out of that area into the region of Tyre and, desiring solitude, entered another house. He wanted to conceal himself from people, but he could not hide. ²⁵ A woman with a sick child found his hiding place and thrust herself into his presence by falling at his feet. ²⁶ The woman was a Syro-

phoenician by birth, and she asked him to make her daughter whole. ²⁷ Jesus responded to her: "A man must first satisfy the needs of his family; it is not customary to take food from the family and give it to strangers or foreigners." ²⁸ The woman agreed. "But," she added, "strangers are given the leftovers from the family table." ²⁹ Jesus said to her, "Because of your response to me, the illness is gone which fragmented your daughter." ³⁰ When this mother returned home, she found her daughter recovered and resting in bed.

Jesus restores hearing and speech

³¹ Jesus moved on from Tyre by way of Sidon to the Sea of Galilee through the region of the Ten Towns. ³² On his journey a person was brought to him who was deaf and could not speak clearly. Those who had brought this man requested Jesus to touch him and make him whole. ³³ Jesus took the fellow's hand and led him away from the crowd. Placing his fingers into the man's ears, he then spat and touched the man's tongue. ³⁴ Jesus lifted his eyes toward the sky and sighed deeply, "Be opened, ears."

³⁵ That very moment the fellow's ears were sensitized and his tongue relaxed so that he spoke clearly. ³⁶ Jesus urged the man and his friends to keep his healing a secret, but the more he made this request, the more they publicized his making persons whole. ³⁷ Those who both experienced and witnessed his healings were astonished beyond description—"He makes everyone whole: he even causes deaf persons to hear and mutes to speak."

A miraculous feeding

8 ¹ During the early days of Jesus' ministry, the crowds that collected around him were huge. On one occasion he called his understudies out of the crowd and spoke these words to them: ² "I feel a deep concern for this crowd because for the three days they have been listening to and traveling with

me, they have had nothing to eat. ³ If I send them home without food, I fear they will pass out along the road because many have come a great distance." ⁴ His understudies responded, "How can you or anyone else provide food out here in this desert?" ⁵ "How many loaves of bread do you have?" Jesus asked. "Seven," they responded. ⁶ "Sit down on the grass," he instructed the crowd. And he took the seven loaves, offered thanks, broke them, and gave the bread to his understudies, who distributed it to the people. ⁷ He did likewise with a few small fish which his understudies found. ⁸ The crowd ate its fill and together they took up seven baskets of leftovers. ⁹ The crowd numbered about four thousand.

¹⁰ After he dismissed them, Jesus entered a boat and went to Dalmanutha. ¹¹ There he again encountered the pious Rule-keepers. They quizzed him, demanding a sign from God to prove his authenticity. Their whole approach irritated Jesus. ¹² He was pained in the depths of his spirit and said, "Why does this generation want an extraordinary occurrence? Honestly I tell you, 'One will not be given you.'" ¹³ With that statement he returned to the boat and departed to the opposite side of the lake.

¹⁴ When the understudies got aboard, they had forgotten to get any food; they had only one loaf of bread. ¹⁵ Jesus began instructing them. "Watch out for the yeast of the pious Rule-keepers, as well as the Revolutionaries." ¹⁶ Hearing the mention of yeast, they immediately concluded he was correcting them for forgetting the bread. ¹⁷ Jesus read their response correctly. "Why are you discussing the bread you forgot? Can't you grasp the symbols I use? Have you become insensitive to your own depths? ¹⁸ You have eyes, don't you see with them? You have ears, don't you hear with them? You have a memory, don't you recall what you have already experienced? ¹⁹ When I broke the five loaves and you distributed them to the five thousand, how many baskets of leftovers did you take up?" "Twelve," they responded. ²⁰ "And what about the

seven loaves that fed the four thousand? How many baskets of leftovers were there?" "Seven," they answered. ²¹ "Then why don't you understand that I am not correcting you for forgetting the bread?" Jesus admonished.

Jesus restores sight

²² In their journeying they came to Bethsaida. Several residents brought a blind man to him for healing. ²³ Jesus took the blind man by the hand and led him outside the town where he wiped his saliva on the man's eyes and touched them with his hands. "Can you see anything?" Jesus asked. ²⁴ Looking up from the ground the man said, "I see people, but they look like trees walking around." ²⁵ Jesus touched his eyes again and asked the man to look up. This time he was made whole and saw everyone in clear perspective. ²⁶ Jesus sent him home with these directions: "Don't go back into town, and don't tell anyone what I have done for you."

Jesus reveals his purpose

²⁷ Jesus left with his understudies and journeyed into the towns of Caesarea Philippi. As they walked along, he asked his followers, "What are the crowds saying about me? Who do they think I am?" ²⁸ They answered, "John the Baptizer; but others say Elijah or one of the old spokesmen for God." ²⁹ "But who do you think I am?" Jesus asked again. Peter responded, "You are the Messiah." ³⁰ And Jesus instructed them, "Do not tell anyone what you have perceived."

³¹ At that point in his training he started telling his understudies that the Representative Man would experience many abuses, be rejected by the rulers, the pious Rulekeepers, and the interpreters of the rules. He stated that they would kill him, but on the third day he would arise. ³² He made this statement very clearly. At once Peter began to reject what Jesus said. ³³ Jesus turned on his heel, looked into the faces of his understudies, and reprimanded Peter: "Don't make such

statements in my presence! You are now being inspired by my Adversary because you evaluate from a personal perspective only and not according to God's intention."

A fulfilled life will be costly

[34] Later on, Jesus signaled the crowd to come in closer to him along with his understudies. He spoke: "If any of you choose to actualize your full potential as I have, you must put to death your pseudo-self, and daily you must say 'no' to your old pattern of living and 'yes' to the new life you see in me. [35] If you try to preserve your life by clinging to your pseudo-self, you will choke it; if you release your life for my sake or for the good news I bring, you will experience the meaning of life. [36] Suppose a person gained the power, wealth, or knowledge the world offers and yet lost himself, his true being, what kind of deal would that be? [37] Picture that possession over against the loss. What do you think that person would give to get his true self back? [38] While I am stating these principles of ultimate significance, I might add that if any of you is embarrassed by your association with me, I will be embarrassed by my association with you at the climax of this world's history."

[9:1] He continued, "Some of you standing here will not die until you have experienced God's presence in tremendous power."

A spiritual transformation

9 [2] About a week later he took the inner circle of his understudies—Peter, James, and John—into a mountain retreat where they were isolated from the crowd. There they experienced Jesus passing through an unexplainable spiritual transformation. [3] Even his clothing seemed to turn white—like a sandy beach at noon. [4] They all experienced the presence of two persons who'd passed away—Moses and Elijah. These

two talked with Jesus. ⁵ So overwhelmed was Peter that he blurted out, "Teacher, this is fantastic! Let's remain here. We could erect three tents—one for you; one for Moses; one for Elijah." ⁶ He didn't know anything else to say because he and the other two were really frightened. ⁷ About that time the shadow of a cloud covered Jesus and the two heavenly characters. A voice seemed to come from the cloud: "This is my much loved Son. Pay attention to what he says."

⁸ When the understudies opened their eyes, they looked around and no one else was present with them but Jesus. ⁹ As they were coming down the mountain, Jesus asked them not to talk about this experience until he had been resurrected. ¹⁰ The request puzzled them and they often discussed among themselves what Jesus had meant by "resurrected."

¹¹ These understudies then asked Jesus, "What do the interpreters of the rules mean when they say, 'Elijah must come back'?" ¹² He answered, "Elijah truly comes back and sets everything in order again before God's Representative Man experiences the depth of his suffering and is apparently wiped out. ¹³ I tell you quite clearly, Elijah has already come back and those in authority did what they had to as was written."

Jesus unites a divided person

¹⁴ When they joined the other followers, Jesus saw that a huge crowd had gathered around them and the interpreters of the rules were interrogating them. ¹⁵ When the crowd saw Jesus, they were struck with awe and ran over to greet him. ¹⁶ "Why are you interrogating my followers?" he demanded of the interpreters. ¹⁷ Before they could respond, a man in the crowd furnished the answer. "Sir, I brought my son to you who at times seems to be separated from himself, as well as being unable to speak. ¹⁸ He seems to be under the power of a separate personality that splits him in two. That other self causes him to foam at the mouth, gnash his teeth, bite

his tongue, and howl like a wild animal. When I asked your followers to make my son whole, they could not."

[19] Jesus said to them all, "O you unbelieving crowd of people, how long must you observe my actions? How long must I endure your lack of faith? Bring your son to me." [20] And they brought the ill lad to Jesus. No sooner was the boy in his presence than he suffered an attack. That 'other' self split off, and the boy fell down on the ground kicking, choking, and screaming. Saliva began running from his mouth. [21] Jesus asked his father, "How long has your son had these seizures?" "Since he was a child," the father responded. [22] "Sometimes this other self tries to destroy him, causing him to fall into the fire and into the lake. So if there is anything you can do, please do it because we desperately need your help." [23] Jesus said, "It is not a question of whether I can do anything; rather, it is a question of whether you can believe. Anything can happen if you can believe." [24] Without a thought the father cried out, "I do believe with part of me—help me believe with the other part."

[25] When Jesus realized the crowd was closing in, he said to the child's separated part, "You insensitive and unresponsive part of this boy, I command you to depart and don't trouble him any more." [26] At those words the boy was thrown into an intense struggle for a few minutes; then the struggle subsided, and the boy relaxed as if he had died. In fact, several in the crowd said, "He is dead." [27] But Jesus took the boy's hand and helped him to his feet. He stood for a moment looking first at Jesus, then at the crowd. [28] Jesus and his understudies left and when they got inside their home, they asked Jesus, "Why couldn't we make that lad whole?" [29] He answered, "Because a situation like this one requires intense prayer; nothing else will affect it."

[30] Jesus and his understudies continued their journeys, passing through Galilee on this trip. Jesus still sought to keep his exact whereabouts a secret. [31] Being aware of the threat

against his life, he kept saying to his understudies, "The Representative Man will be handed over to his enemies and finally executed by them. After his execution he will experience resurrection on the third day." [32] His understudies did not grasp the meaning of "execution" and "resurrection" and were afraid to ask him about it.

The child symbol

[33] When they got to Capernaum, they entered a house and Jesus asked, "What were you arguing about on the trip?" [34] They sat in silence because on the way they had been arguing about position—who would have the chief place. [35] Jesus paused, got the attention of the twelve, and said, "If you want to be first, accept being behind everyone and servant of everyone." [36] He illustrated this puzzling statement using the symbol of a child. Picking up a little child in his arms, Jesus said, [37] "When you accept a little child into your life, you accept me; and in accepting me, you accept the One who sent me."

[38] John, one of the understudies, said, "Teacher, we observed a man who is not an understudy making persons whole in your name. Because he is not an understudy and consequently unqualified, we told him to stop." [39] "Don't stop him," Jesus said. "A person cannot heal in my name and later discount me. [40] If a person does not declare himself against us, he is with us. [41] Anyone who shares with you the least of gifts like a cup of water because you are Christpersons, I tell you the truth—he will not lose his investment. [42] Now, back to the child symbol. Whoever acts destructively toward a child in the faith, it would be better for that person to be executed than to go on functioning destructively.

[43] "If you do things with your hands that thwart your life, it is better to cut your hands off than to block the flow of your life. It is better to live without hands [44] than to distort the purpose of your life and live in utter despair and regret.

[45] The same principle applies to your foot leading you astray [46] with the loss and regret that would occur. [47] Likewise, the same judgment applies to the eye and its power to distort your perspective [48] and the grief and loss that results from it. [49] Everyone will experience testing in the things he does, in the places he goes, and in how he sees things; but the meaning of each decision made according to the purpose of God will be preserved. [50] Salt makes food taste good. If salt loses its taste, it can't season any longer. Keep your lives full of salt and live in unity with each other."

Jesus discusses marriage

10 [1] Jesus continued to move about from place to place, and in his journey he entered into Judea from the farther side of the Jordan River. When his presence was known, the crowds gathered and he instructed them as he always did. [2] In the course of his teaching a group of pious Rulekeepers came to him, asking, "Is it proper for a man to renounce his responsibility to his wife?" (They were setting a trap for him.) [3] His response: "What did Moses, your rulemaker, say about that issue?" [4] They said, "Moses permitted us to write a letter of dismissal announcing our release from all responsibility." [5] Jesus said, "Because of your insensitivity to each other, Moses gave you this rule. [6] God in the beginning made man, then woman, [7] and he intended for a man to disjoin himself from his father and mother and unite himself to his wife. [8] When this type of union occurs, these two persons function harmoniously, as if they were one person; [9] when God so joins two persons, no one should sever their relation."

[10] When they went inside the house, his understudies asked him for clarification on the subject. [11] He said, "If anyone severs his union with his wife and marries another woman, he is unfaithful to the union God gave them. [12] If a woman renounces her union with her husband and marries another man, she is unfaithful to the union God created."

Jesus affirms childlikeness

¹³ Again parents in the crowd brought small children to Jesus requesting him to touch and hold them. His understudies criticized these parents for taking Jesus' time. ¹⁴ When Jesus realized what his understudies were doing, he was disturbed by their behavior. "Permit these small children easy access to me, and do not make it difficult for them because they participate in the Spirit dimension. ¹⁵ I tell you the truth, if a person does not open himself to the Spirit dimension as a child does, he will not participate in it at all." ¹⁶ Then he took the children in his arms and touched them with his hands, affirming their special place with God.

Warning against wealth

¹⁷ Later when he was on another trip, a man came running up to him, fell on his knees, and asked, "Good teacher, tell me how I may receive life age after age." ¹⁸ Jesus replied, "Why do you address me as 'good' teacher? Only God is good. ¹⁹ Anyway, in response to your question, you know the rules for living. Do not commit adultery, nor kill, nor steal, nor lie, nor deceive. Respect your parents." ²⁰ The young man countered, "Teacher, from my earliest recollection I have faithfully observed these rules, but this has not given life to me." ²¹ Aware of the intense struggle raging in the man, Jesus gazed into his eyes and cared deeply for him. "Only one thing blocks your experience of real life: return to your home, sell all your possessions, and give the proceeds to the poor. Then give yourself to me." ²² The young fellow felt depressed when he thought about Jesus' directive. He went home distraught because he was quite wealthy.

²³ After he had gotten out of hearing, Jesus said to his understudies, "It is very difficult for persons of wealth to enter the Spirit dimension!" ²⁴ His understudies were shocked at his statement. Jesus repeated his message. "My babes in

understanding, those who trust in wealth have difficulty entering the Spirit dimension. ²⁵ A camel can crawl through the low gate in the city wall easier than a rich man can enter the Spirit dimension." ²⁶ With this emphasis they were shocked out of their wits. Questioning among themselves they asked, "If the wealthy have such difficulty, who can rightly relate to God?" ²⁷ Jesus said, "It is not possible for persons in their own strength to enter the Spirit dimension, but when God takes the initiative everything is possible."

²⁸ In response Peter said, "What about us? We have given up everything to be your understudies and to participate in your ministry." ²⁹ Jesus said, "I tell you the truth, no person will leave behind his possessions, his house and lot, and his relatives—like his brothers or sisters or father or mother or wife or children—on my behalf, or on behalf of the good news, and go unrewarded. ³⁰ In this present time he will receive a hundred times what he gave up in material possessions like a house and lot, and in addition he will have relatives as intimate as father or mother, brother or sister, wife or children—plus authentic life age after age. ³¹ Many who have commanded attention and exercised power in this age will go unrecognized in the age which is dawning; and many who have been unrecognized will be prominent."

Journey to fulfillment

³² One day as the understudies were traveling along the road to Jerusalem with Jesus, they had an awesome experience which shattered their consciousness and left them frightened. This occurred when Jesus told them what was about to happen to him. ³³ He explained, "We are on the way to Jerusalem, where the Representative Man will be handed over to the religious leaders and the interpreters of the rules and they will sentence him to die. They will then hand him over to the non-Jews ³⁴ who will abuse him in every way imaginable—verbally, mentally, and physically—and they will kill him, and on the third day he will experience resurrection."

[35] As they continued the trip, James and John, Zebedee's sons, came to Jesus with a request: "Teacher, give us the thing that we most deeply desire." [36] "What is that?" Jesus queried. [37] They answered, "We want to have places of importance when you begin wielding your power and authority." [38] Jesus said, "You really don't understand me or the nature of my authority. Can you stand firm in your commitment as I do? Can you accept the consequences of your choices as I will?" [39] And they said, "We can." Jesus responded, "You will indeed stick with your commitment, and you will also suffer the consequences of that decision. [40] However, it is not my prerogative to designate the seats of importance because they have already been designated."

[41] When the other understudies overheard what was being discussed, they were furious with James and John. [42] Jesus gathered them all together and said, "You know that in the authority structures which the non-Jews have established, the persons of prominence rule those of lesser importance and the chain of command stretches from the highest to the lowest. [43] That order of authority is not appropriate for you. If you want great importance, you must be a minister. [44] If you want the highest position, you must serve every person. [45] The Representative Man did not come to rule over persons but to serve them, and to give himself that others could be freed to become what God intended."

Jesus opens eyes

[46] One day in their travels Jesus and the understudies came to Jericho. As they left the city, accompanied by a crowd, they approached a blind beggar sitting by the road, Bartimaeus, the son of Timaeus. [47] When someone in the crowd told him that Jesus of Nazareth was passing by, he began to call out, "Jesus, son of David, please help me!" [48] Numerous persons in the crowd told him to be quiet, but Bartimaeus shouted even louder: "Jesus, son of David, please help me!" [49] Jesus stopped. He told the understudies to bring the blind

man to him. They called out to the blind man, "Take courage. Come over here. He wants to see you." ⁵⁰ The blind man pulled off his wrap, got up, and made his way toward Jesus. ⁵¹ Jesus asked, "What do you want me to do for you?" The blind man answered, "Sir, I want to be able to see." ⁵² "Now fulfill your destiny," Jesus said. "Your trust has made you a whole person." At that instant he began to see and he followed Jesus, fulfilling his destiny.

Final preparation

11 ¹ Later on when they were headed for Jerusalem, they stopped at Bethphage and Bethany near the Mount of Olives. Jesus selected two understudies and ² gave them those instructions: "Go into the next village and at the edge of the village you will find a colt tied which has never been ridden. Untie him and bring him. ³ If anyone asks why you are taking the colt, just say, 'Our leader needs him.' And, with that reply they will ask no more questions."

⁴ The two understudies entered the village and saw the colt beside the door of a house located at the crossroads. When they untied him, ⁵ certain persons standing there asked, "Why are you untying the colt?" ⁶ They responded as Jesus had told them, and the questioners said nothing else. ⁷˙⁸ They brought the colt to Jesus and after they had spread their clothes on the road, others cut branches from the trees and spread them across the road. ⁹ The crowd around him began to chant: "Celebrate life! Celebrate! Blessings on the one who represents the Lord. ¹⁰ Blessings on the order initiated by our father David, which is coming in this man. Praise to God in the highest." ¹¹ In this fashion Jesus entered Jerusalem and went directly to God's house. After he had examined carefully the state of affairs in the house of God, he returned to Bethany with his twelve understudies about sundown.

¹² The next day as Jesus and his understudies returned from Bethany, he was hungry. ¹³ In the distance he saw a fig tree,

and walked over to it hoping to find some fruit. However, he found nothing but leaves because the fruit was not yet in season. ¹⁴ In response to the tree's fruitlessness Jesus said to it, "No one will ever eat fruit from your branches." His understudies heard his pronouncement and felt there was a message in his statement.

¹⁵ After that episode they went on into the city. Jesus entered God's house and promptly began disrupting the activities of the businesses operating there—forcing out the money-changers and sellers of doves. ¹⁶ He also blocked the transport of merchandise into or out of God's house. ¹⁷ He explained the reason for his action: "In our record God has said, 'My house will be described as a house of prayer for all persons without regard for national origin,' but you have converted God's house into a market place of inflated prices."

¹⁸ When the interpreters of the rules and the pious Rule-keepers heard his condemnation, they immediately began to plot to get Jesus killed. They wanted to kill him because the crowds were captivated by both his teaching and his actions. ¹⁹ About sundown he returned to Bethany.

Desire and prayer

²⁰ The next morning on their way back to the city, Jesus and his understudies passed by the same fig tree and noted that from root to leaf it was withered. ²¹ Peter, recalling the incident of the preceding day, said, "Teacher, look at this fig tree you spoke to yesterday; it's all withered." ²² Jesus said, "Trust in God. ²³ Truly, anyone who speaks to that mountain yonder saying, 'Dump yourself in the lake,' and does not become separated from the statement he makes—that person will actualize his statement. When anyone's expression in prayer is congruent with his inner being, his desire will be actualized. ²⁴ Because of this principle, when you discover your soul's deepest desires, state them in your prayers, and consider them to have occurred—they will!

²⁵ When you are making these statements which spring from your innermost being, forgive any person against whom you have a grudge so that your desires don't get ensnared by your grudges. When you forgive others, your Father will forgive you, and your relationship with him will be positive."*

The authority of John

²⁷ By the time this discussion ended, they were inside the city. As Jesus walked into the house of God, he was accosted by the interpreters of the rules and the religious officials. ²⁸ They asked, "What right do you have to disrupt the activities going on here? Who gave you that right, anyway?" ²⁹ "Before I tell you why I have this right and who gave it to me, let me ask you a question," Jesus responded. ³⁰ "Did God give John the right to baptize, or was his action merely human?" ³¹ They went into a huddle and argued about their answer: "If we say God gave him the right, he will ask why we didn't respond to him. ³² If we say it was merely human, the crowd will attack us because they believe he was commissioned by God." ³³ Finally they said to Jesus, "We can't answer." Jesus replied, "Neither will I tell you why I have the right to do these things."

A story about rebellion

12 ¹ Once again Jesus taught his understudies with a story. "A certain man founded a winery: he did everything from planting the grapes to selecting tenants for the enterprise. Then he left. ² At the time when the grapes were to be harvested, he sent a representative to collect on his investment. ³ But the tenants beat the owner's representative and sent him away empty-handed. ⁴ A second time the owner sent a representative and again the tenants attacked him and left him bruised and bleeding. ⁵ The owner sent one representative

---

* Verse 26 is not found in the best manuscripts.

after the other, and those in charge of his property turned each one back, beating some and killing others. ⁶ The owner had only one son, a boy whom he loved dearly. Last of all, he sent this son, thinking, 'Surely, they will respect my son and respond to him.' ⁷ They responded, all right. They said among themselves, 'This son is the heir; let's kill him and the winery will be ours.' ⁸ So they imprisoned him, then killed him, and threw his body out."

⁹ Jesus asked his understudies: "What will the owner of the winery do? Why, he himself will come with force to expel those unreliable tenants and replace them with other tenants." ¹⁰ He continued, "Do you recall the old saying, 'The stone which the mason continually rejected has now become the most significant stone in the building'? ¹¹ This is how God works and it produces awe in us when we perceive it." ¹² Though the Jewish leaders wanted desperately to jail Jesus, they couldn't be too obvious because they feared the crowds. They were fully aware that the symbolic story was an indictment of them, but being helpless for the moment, they left.

God and civil authority

¹³ The pious Rulekeepers and Herod's loyal supporters joined forces and sent agents to gather information to indict him. ¹⁴ Their remarks to him were in the guise of affirmation: "Teacher, you are an authentic person unaffected by the reactions of other persons; you are not seeking to get the approval of others, but you authentically set forth the way of God. Tell us, is it God's will for us to pay taxes to Rome? ¹⁵ Should we pay or not?" Jesus recognized their intent and responded, "Why do you place me in such a bind? Hand me a coin, if you will." ¹⁶ His opponents handed him one. He then asked, "Whose picture and inscription are stamped on it?" "Caesar's," they replied. ¹⁷ "Give to Caesar what is Caesar's and to God what is God's," Jesus answered. His response shook them by unmasking their sinister motives.

Meaning of resurrection

¹⁸ After this encounter the ruling aristocrats, who denied the resurrection, sought to expose him. ¹⁹ "Teacher, Moses, as you know, told us that if a man marries and then dies, his brother must marry his wife and father children in his stead. ²⁰ We have on record a case in which there were seven brothers. The first married, then died before his wife conceived. ²¹ The second brother married his brother's wife; he, too, died having no child. The third brother met the same fate. ²² In succession, all seven married the woman and died without having a child. Finally, the woman died. ²³ Here is our question: In the resurrection, to whom shall she be united because in this life each was united to her?"

²⁴ Jesus answered, "Your logic is faulty and your spiritual perception is dull; are you unaware of both God's purpose and his power? ²⁵ When these persons experience resurrection, they will not be in a married state, but more nearly like God's special messengers who live in his presence. ²⁶ With regard to the question of resurrection, don't you recall what God said to Moses through the bush that burned? 'I am God of Abraham and God of Isaac and God of Jacob.' ²⁷ God is not the God of nothing, but of something; not the God of nonbeing, but of true being. No, you are mistaken."

Rules for living

²⁸ One of the interpreters of the rules felt the impact of Jesus' answer to these ruling aristocrats, and he himself posed a question to Jesus: "What is the most important rule for living?" ²⁹ Immediately Jesus responded, "The most important rule is, 'Listen, Israel, the Lord our God is one; ³⁰ and you are to love the Lord your God with all your feelings, with all your inner being, and with all your intelligence to the fullest of your capacity.' This is the most important rule. ³¹ Next in importance is the directive to 'love every person just as you love yourself.' No directive from God is greater than these two."

³² The interpreter of the rules said, "Teacher, you have really answered my inquiry because there truly is only one God. There are no others. ³³ To love him with your whole being—emotions, intellect, spiritual depth, to the limit of these capacities—and to love every other person as intensely as you love yourself is a directive which supersedes every other rule or ritual." ³⁴ When Jesus recognized his keen spiritual perception, he said, "You are on the fringe of the Spirit dimension." And this ended the questioning for that day.

Warning against legalism

³⁵ One day when Jesus was teaching in God's house, he asked, "Why do the interpreters of the rules claim that the Messiah will be David's son? ³⁶ Recall that David, inspired by the Spirit, described his relationship to the Messiah: 'The Lord spoke to the Messiah, "Sit here beside me until I conquer all that opposes you." ' ³⁷ If David in his lifetime confessed the Messiah, how can the Messiah be his child!"

The man on the street listened to his teaching with enthusiasm. ³⁸ Jesus continued, "Watch out for those professional interpreters of the rules who enjoy displaying their religion externally by the clothes they wear, the greetings they exchange, ³⁹ the places they sit in worship, or at a party. ⁴⁰ These persons prey on the weak and cover their greed with long prayers. Their own behavior condemns them to superficiality and meaninglessness."

⁴¹ Jesus then sat down beside the collection box and observed the contributions which were being made. He noted a number of rich persons making large contributions. ⁴² About that time a poverty-stricken widow came up and dropped in a couple of coins worth about a nickel. ⁴³ Jesus then called his understudies and said, "This poor widow has given more than all these wealthy contributors. ⁴⁴ They have given a token contribution from their abundance, but she out of her poverty has contributed her last cent."

Calamity forecast

13 ¹ As they were leaving God's house, one of the understudies said, "Teacher, notice all these huge buildings, how they are constructed!" ² Jesus responded, "Do you see how large these buildings are and how well they are constructed? Not one stone will be left in place; each will be shattered and tumble down."

³ As he was sitting in the Mount of Olives adjacent to God's house, Peter, James, John, and Andrew said, "Tell us when this calamity will occur and what will signal its approach." ⁵ Jesus answered, "Be very careful to whom you listen. ⁶ Numerous persons will pretend to be the Messiah and will convince many followers. ⁷ Before the final consummation you will have war after war. Do not permit these to panic you because strife will come before the consummation of history. ⁸ During this time there will be misunderstanding and conflict between nations, rulers will oppose each other, the earth will quiver, persons will starve; many will suffer—and this is only the beginning.

⁹ "Be aware of your loyalty. Your enemies will haul you into court; they will beat you in the places of worship; they will expose you before the rulers of the nations requiring you to tell your story which will accuse the rulers. ¹⁰ Before the fulfillment of God's purpose, the good news must be told in every nation. ¹¹ When they force you to tell your story before these dignitaries, don't rehearse your speech. At the moment you will speak spontaneously; what you say will be inspired by the Holy Spirit, and it will not feel as though *you* are saying the words. ¹² During this period of upheaval, family loyalty will break down completely, so much so that brothers will testify against each other, parents will testify against their own children, and even children will testify against their parents. This disloyalty will result in the death of their family

members. ¹³ During this time of social and political upheaval, you will yourselves be the object of wrath because you confess your loyalty to me. But every person who remains loyal to me throughout the upheaval will be delivered.

¹⁴ "Now regarding the utter destruction of this house of God, whenever you see the most irreverent, unholy act imaginable transpiring in this consecrated place, if you are in Judea, evacuate the city and hide in the mountains. ¹⁵ Should you be on the roof of your dwelling, don't take time to go inside and pack your goods. ¹⁶ Should you be cultivating your crop, don't even pick up your shirt. ¹⁷ This time of calamity will be worse for pregnant women and mothers of small children because they cannot travel fast. ¹⁸ Do hope and pray that your escape is not in the rainy season. ¹⁹ During the time I am describing, people will experience greater suffering than at any period since God created the earth. ²⁰ And unless God intervenes to shorten that period, not a person will survive. Yet, for the sake of those persons whom he chose, he will intervene and they will survive.

The climax of history

²¹ " During this era of such intense pain and suffering when men will be looking for an escape, if anyone says 'here is the Messiah who will deliver us' . . . or 'Look, he is over there' . . . don't believe the report. ²² Pseudo-Messiahs and phony witnesses will appear and will deceive many persons with their so-called miracles and signs. If such were possible, they would turn God's chosen people off the track. ²³ You must remember that I have forecast all these things.

²⁴ "In the days following this extreme period of suffering, you will note signs in the heavenly bodies: the sun will go into an eclipse and so will the moon; ²⁵ stars will appear to fall from the sky, and the whole universe will appear disordered. ²⁶ After all this occurs, those who survive will recognize the reap-

pearance of God's Representative Man who will reorder all the powers in the universe. ²⁷ As his first priority, he will assemble God's people from everywhere.

²⁸ "You can learn an important lesson from the fig tree symbol. When the fig tree buds and shoots out leaves, you know that the dry season approaches. ²⁹ When you see all these things happening, you can be confident that the Ultimate Fulfillment is approaching. ³⁰ Truly, this generation will experience all the things I have described. ³¹ Everything else in this world may become null and void, but the truth I declare will not; it will stand.

³² "No one knows the era, much less the year, when all creation will be fulfilled, not God's special agents, not his Son; only the Father knows when the fulfillment will come. ³³ Be aware that there is an end to all things—a fulfillment for everything. Be sensitive to God's Spirit and keep your lives open to him because you do not know when the fulfillment will come. ³⁴ God's Representative Man is like a traveler en route to a distant country. In preparation for the trip he delegated responsibilities to his employees, instructing them to be diligent. ³⁵ 'Be on the alert,' he said, 'because you do not know the exact time of my return. I may return in the evening, at midnight, or early in the morning at the break of dawn. ³⁶ You must be diligent in your task and faithful to your responsibility because you do not know when you will be asked to account for yourself. So don't go to sleep on the job!'" ³⁷ Jesus continued, "What I am instructing you understudies, I mean for every person. Be responsible in the management of your life."

Act now

14 ¹ A couple of days later when Jesus attended the Jewish celebration of the nation's Exodus from Egypt, the top religious leaders and the interpreters of the rules plotted how they could arrest him and put him to death. ² But considering the crowd at the celebration, they decided to wait to avoid a riot.

³ About that time Jesus was having dinner in Bethany (a village near Jerusalem) at the home of Simon, a man he had cured of leprosy. While he was eating, a woman with a flask of perfume entered the house, broke the flask, and poured the perfume over Jesus' head. ⁴ Several table guests were angered by her interruption and also by the waste. "Why," they demanded, "have you squandered this expensive perfume? ⁵ You could have sold it for a hundred dollars or more and contributed the money to the poor." They continued to badmouth her.

⁶ "Be quiet," Jesus commanded. "Stop your criticism. Her behavior is commendable. ⁷ You will always have opportunity to assist the poor, and you can respond to their needs when you choose; but I will not always be here. ⁸ This woman responded to me while she had the opportunity. In fact, she has forecast my death by preparing my body for burial. ⁹ And, wherever the good news is told throughout the world, special mention of this gift to me will be made."

The betrayal contract

¹⁰ Then Judas Iscariot, one of the twelve understudies, approached the top religious leaders and agreed to tell them where Jesus was and to identify him personally so there would be no mistake. ¹¹ When the leaders heard his proposal, they were pleased and agreed to pay him for his service. So Judas began looking for the time and place he could most easily point Jesus out to them.

Preparation for a celebration

¹² On the first day of preparation for the celebration of the Exodus from Egypt, the understudies asked Jesus, "Where do you want us to prepare the food for our celebration of the Exodus?" ¹³ Jesus said to two of them, "Go into the city; you

will meet a man carrying a pitcher of water. ¹⁴ Follow him into whichever house he enters and say to the owner of that house, 'Our Teacher asks, "Where is the guestroom in which he will celebrate the Exodus with his understudies?" ' ¹⁵ The owner will then show you a large room on the top floor of his house. It will have the necessities for our celebration so you can go ahead and prepare for it." ¹⁶ With those instructions the two understudies departed, entered the city, and found everything as Jesus had told them. They prepared for the celebration.

God's new covenant

¹⁷ After sundown Jesus and the other understudies came to the place which had been prepared. ¹⁸ While they were eating, Jesus said, "One of you understudies now eating with me will hand me over to the religious leaders." ¹⁹ That statement unleashed all their fears and one by one they asked him, "Is it I? Is it I?" until each had asked him.

²⁰ Jesus answered, "It is one of the twelve men eating this meal with me. ²¹ The Representative Man will die as was expected by the ancients, but the man who precipitates his death will bear an unbearable burden! Better for him that he had never been born."

²² While they were celebrating, Jesus took a loaf of bread and broke it into pieces for them after he verbally acknowledged God as the source of the bread. He said, "Eat this bread, it is my body." ²³ He took the goblet in his hands, acknowledging God as the source of the wine. He passed it among them, and each drank. ²⁴ He explained their symbolic action: "This is my blood signifying the new relation between God and man. ²⁵ Truly I will not celebrate with you again until that era when history is fulfilled, and we celebrate together the Ultimate Fulfillment of all things."

²⁶ With that declaration the group burst into singing. Afterwards, they got up from the table and headed for the Mount of Olives. ²⁷ On the way Jesus began to forecast what they could expect: "All of you will be ashamed of your relation

to me this very night. One of the ancients has described your behavior: When the parent dies, the children go to pieces. ²⁸ After the ordeal of the next few days I will experience resurrection, and I will meet you in Galilee."

²⁹ Peter, still recalling Jesus' prediction, said, "If everyone else is ashamed of his relation with you, I won't be." ³⁰ "Why, Peter," Jesus said, "during this very night before the rooster crows announcing the dawn of a new day, you will deny your connection with me three times." ³¹ Peter was adamant in his pledge of loyalty. "If the enemies kill me along with you, even then I won't deny my relation to you." And, all the others pledged themselves as strongly as Peter.

Jesus struggles in prayer

³² About that time they arrived at Gethsemane. Jesus said to the understudies, "Wait here while I pray," ³³ and he invited Peter, James, and John to pray with him. They observed Jesus' stress and intense struggle. ³⁴ Jesus said to them, "I feel grief in the depths of my being as I face my death. Stay close to me and share my pain."

³⁵ After making this request he took a few steps forward and fell to his knees, praying to avoid the agony he was facing. ³⁶ He said, "Father, you are the source of every possibility. Remove this agony from me if, according to your purpose, that is possible. However, more than I want what I am feeling, I desire for your purpose to be fulfilled." ³⁷ After that struggle in prayer, he came back to his three understudies and found them asleep. "Peter, are you asleep, too? Could you not participate in my suffering for just one hour? ³⁸ Be aware of the conflict between what you feel at the moment and what you choose as the higher good. Ask God to help you so that this conflict does not destroy you. Truly, your spirit is sensitive to the higher good, but your physical needs dull the spirit's perception."

³⁹ A second time he went away and prayed the same prayer. ⁴⁰ When he returned, he again found them asleep. When he

[149

awakened them, they didn't know what to say. [41] After praying a third time, he found them asleep again. This time he let them sleep on. "Enjoy your moment of rest. My struggle is over. My time of death has come. God's Representative Man will be turned over to the establishment. [42] Get up. Let's go. The one turning me in is now on his way here."

Betrayal and arrest

[43] While he was speaking those very words, Judas, one of his understudies, came up. He was accompanied by a crowd waving sticks and swords. These had been sent by the establishment: the religious leaders, the national leaders, and the interpreters of the rules. [44] Judas had given the crowd a sign: "Whomever I kiss is your man. Capture him and take him away without harming him." [45] As soon as Judas arrived, he went directly to Jesus: "Teacher! Teacher!" And he kissed him.

[46] The leaders took Jesus into custody. [47] One of his understudies grabbed a sword and sliced off the ear of an employee of a prominent religious official. [48] Then Jesus addressed the mob: "Have you come to arrest a criminal—with your staves and swords? [49] Every day I have been in the house of God teaching you, and you didn't think I was a criminal then. But now I must fulfill my destiny." [50] All his followers and recent admirers abandoned him.

[51] In the mob there was a young man with a linen cloth wrapped around his body (presumably he was responding sympathetically to Jesus). Several young men in the mob, noting his response, grabbed his linen cloth, [52] but he broke free and ran away in the nude.

The charge of blasphemy

[53] The mob took Jesus directly to their top religious official. He had already called a meeting of the decision-makers —the religious and national leaders and the interpreters of the rules. [54] While all the other understudies ran away and hid,

Peter followed along on the fringe of the mob. He went right up to the mansion of the religious official and sat down at a fire to warm himself with the servants.

⁵⁵ Inside, the leaders were questioning the mob that had apprehended Jesus—they had to find someone who would testify against him, and they had difficulty finding a substantial witness. ⁵⁶ As they questioned various witnesses, they found them in conflict, one saying one thing and another something which contradicted it. ⁵⁷ At last they found two who agreed in their testimony. ⁵⁸ "We heard this man say, 'I will demolish this house of God which you have constructed with your labor, and in just three days I will replace it without any labor at all.'" ⁵⁹ But even these two were not in perfect agreement as to his exact words.

⁶⁰ The top religious leader stood up and addressed Jesus, "Don't you have anything to say about these allegations? How do you explain your words?" ⁶¹ Calm and collected, Jesus made no response. The official pressed Jesus again, "Are you the Messiah, the Son of the one we worship?" ⁶² "Yes, I am," Jesus answered. "You will see for yourself the Representative Man expressing the authority of God and radiating the energy of that dimension of being."

⁶³ With that clear witness from Jesus' own lips, the religious leader said, "What need have we for other witnesses? ⁶⁴ You have heard this man admit that he is God's Son and special representative among men." The council agreed with the verdict and sentenced him to death. ⁶⁵ With the sentencing the mob began spitting on him; soon his face was covered and they slapped him and pushed him around. They mockingly said, "Preach to us more! Tell us more of your fantasy!" Even the guards began slapping him around.

Peter deserts the cause

⁶⁶ While Peter was sitting around the fire in the courtyard, a maid approached him. ⁶⁷ As Peter sat there warming himself, she said, "Weren't you with Jesus of Nazareth?" ⁶⁸ Startled,

[151

Peter answered, "I certainly was not! I don't know what you are talking about." As he got up and walked away, he heard a rooster crow. ⁶⁹Another maid recognized him and said to the men standing beside Peter, "This man is one of Jesus' followers." ⁷⁰Again Peter said, "I am not." In a few minutes those men said, "Certainly you are one of them; you must be because you speak with a Galilean accent." ⁷¹He began to curse and swear. I do not know this man." ⁷²Once again Peter heard the rooster crow. And he remembered Jesus' prediction —"Before the rooster crows twice, you will deny me three times." The memory of the words and the realization of what he had done filled him with such regret that he burst into tears.

Jesus condemned to death

15 ¹Early the next morning, the religious and political leaders held a conference to decide the fate of Jesus. They decided to hand him over to Pilate, Rome's representative. ²Based on the information the Jews had given him, Pilate asked, "Are you a ruler of these persons?" Jesus responded, "It's as your question suggests." ³The religious leaders trumped up a number of charges, but Jesus replied to none of them. ⁴Pilate said, "Aren't you going to defend yourself? Listen to the charges they are bringing against you." ⁵This time Jesus did not respond to his prodding. His silence in the face of these accusations amazed and stunned Pilate.

⁶Each year during the feast it had become customary for Pilate to free a prisoner selected by the Jews themselves. ⁷Among the political prisoners whom Pilate had captured was a man named Barabbas who had taken part in a revolt against Rome and had killed several persons. ⁸Because of their expectation, the crowd began to chant for the annual release of a prisoner. ⁹Pilate asked, "Do you wish me to release your ruler—the one who calls himself your king?" ¹⁰He was aware that the religious leaders had falsified their charges and that

fear was their real reason for taking him into custody. ¹¹ While the crowd was considering this option, the religious leaders told them to request the release of Barabbas. ¹² "What do you suggest that I do with this man who claims to be your king?" he asked. ¹³ With one voice they began to chant: "Kill him. Kill him." ¹⁴ "Why do you demand his death?" Pilate asked. "What has he done wrong?" But all he heard from the crowd was "Kill him, kill him."

¹⁵ Pilate chose to appease the crowd rather than respond to his own conscience, so he released Barabbas and instructed his officer to beat Jesus and kill him. ¹⁶ The soldiers led him to the courtyard of the governor's residence where they got the whole company together. ¹⁷ For sport they put a purple robe on Jesus and formed a crown of thorns and put it on his head. ¹⁸ The soldiers began to dance and clap, shouting, "Hail to the chief, the king of the Jews!" ¹⁹ One struck him on the head with a cane, others spat on him, and each took his turn kneeling before him in mock homage. ²⁰ When they had ridiculed him to their satisfaction, they stripped the robe off him and redressed him in his own clothes. Then they led him out of the courtyard to kill him. ²¹ As they led him out, they drafted a passerby, Simon, a visitor from Cyrene (father of Alexander and Rufus), to carry the cross.

The execution

²² They marched all the way to the place called Golgotha —so named because it resembled a skull. ²³ Before the execution they offered Jesus a mixture of wine and myrrh to lessen the pain, but he refused the sedatives. ²⁴ And when they had nailed him to the cross, they took the clothes he had been wearing and gambled for them.

²⁵ They nailed him to the cross at 9:00 A.M. ²⁶ So that all would know the crime for which he was being executed, they hung this inscription on his cross: "the King of the Jews" (because that was the charge brought against him). ²⁷ At the

time of Jesus' execution, two thieves were also being executed, one on his left and another on his right.*

²⁹ And the spectators who passed by shook their heads and pointed their fingers at Jesus. They ridiculed and mocked him, saying, "You were going to destroy God's house and rebuild it in three days. ³⁰ Why don't you do something easier —like freeing yourself from the cross?" ³¹ The religious officials and interpreters of the rules who were present to observe the execution said mockingly to each other, "He could set others free, but he can't free himself." ³² They continued to jeer, "Let the Messiah, the King of Israel, come down off the cross and when we see that, we will believe." In addition to the mob of spectators, the thieves being executed taunted him.

³³ After three hours (about noon) it became dark throughout the countryside until 3:00 P.M. ³⁴ At 3 o'clock Jesus cried out, "My God, my God, why have you left me alone?" ³⁵ Misunderstanding his words, the spectators said, "He's calling on Elijah, the prophet who went up into heaven." ³⁶ One of the spectators filled a sponge with vinegar and pushed it up to his mouth with a reed, saying, "Let's see if Elijah will come to free him." ³⁷ From the depths of his being, Jesus cried out in agony and died. ³⁸ And the curtain was torn which separated the people from the holiest portion of God's house—a sign that his death had unveiled the mystery of God.

³⁹ Those persons around the cross responded to his death in a variety of ways. A soldier standing by said, "This man must have been the Son of God." ⁴⁰,⁴¹ At a distance a group of women who had followed Jesus observed his death. Among them were Mary Magdalene; Mary, the mother of James and Joses; and Salome (the one who identified with him in Galilee and served him there). Also in the group were a number of other women who had come to Jerusalem with him.

---

* Verse 28 is not found in the best manuscripts.

Jesus' entombment

⁴² The day of execution was Friday, the day prior to the Jewish Sabbath. Because Jesus could not be left on the cross on the Sabbath, ⁴³ Joseph from Arimathea, who was a distinguished member of the council and was seeking to enter the Spirit dimension, courageously went to Pilate and earnestly requested custody of Jesus' body. ⁴⁴ Pilate was amazed that he had already been executed, and he sent for a soldier to confirm that Jesus was indeed dead. ⁴⁵ With the soldier's confirmation he released the body to Joseph. ⁴⁶ Joseph then bought an expensive piece of linen, took Jesus down from the cross, wrapped him in the linen, and laid him in a grave (the grave was actually a cave cut out of a rock); then he sealed the cave with a larger stone. ⁴⁷ Two of the aforementioned women observed the proceedings, Mary Magdalene and the other Mary.

Jesus' resurrection

16 ¹ When the Jewish day of rest ended, the trio of Mary Magdalene, Mary (James' mother), and Salome decided to buy spices and herbs to put on Jesus' body. ² Very early Sunday morning they came out to the cave in which Jesus had been buried. It was about sunup. ³ As they walked along, they began to wonder who they would get to roll away the stone from the cave's entrance.

⁴ When they arrived, they saw that the stone had already been removed. This raised further questions for them because the stone was so heavy. ⁵ They went on into the cave in which Jesus had been entombed. Sitting there on the right side was a young man dressed in white. The women were startled and frightened. ⁶ The young man spoke: "Do not be afraid! You are looking for Jesus who was from Nazareth, the one who was executed. He is no longer here. He has been resurrected. Look over there where he was lying. ⁷ You go back and tell

[155

his understudies, including Peter, that he is going to Galilee to meet you. You will see him there as he told you." [8] With these words the women hastily ran out of the tomb, still shaking with fear and amazement. They told no one what had happened because they were frightened.*

---

* The rest of this chapter is not found in the oldest manuscripts.